Japanese Management

This book provides a new understanding of the constellations of logics in Japanese management practices in Asia and the West. Through comparative ethnographic case studies of a Japanese multinational corporation (MNC), the book explores the cultural meanings of family, corporation, market and religion logics at each subsidiary's site in Thailand, Taiwan, Belgium and the United States.

In doing so, the book defines cultural space through an institutional logic approach. It argues that logics are culturally interpreted, which can impose a serious limitation on the institutional logic approach based on the analysis of Western society. It reveals that Japanese 'family' logics and Theravada Buddhism in Asia are strengthening each other and this directly supports the presupposition of amplification. It further elaborates on the ongoing constellations of logics that are continuously formed in relation to geographical contexts. The book also explains that the boundaries of organisational communities are not automatically formed by Japanese expatriates but constructed through the actors' profiles, which, in turn, raises their importance.

Therefore, this book is a must-read for researchers, managers and anyone interested in Japanese MNCs.

Hitoshi Iwashita (PhD, MBA) is an academic researcher and management consultant in terms of international management, cross cultural management and leadership, managerial work, strategy execution, and organisation studies. He taught organisational behaviour at Cardiff Business School and GLOBIS Management School. Before becoming a doctoral researcher, he was an independent management consultant, a representative at Value Associates Inc. He completed an International MBA from IE Business School, and received a PhD in Business and Management from Cardiff Business School. His continuing interest lies in developing practice oriented research and education in cross cultural management.

'This book examines Japanese multinational subsidiaries as hybrid forms of organisation, bridging national institutional contexts and cultures. Taking an ethnographic approach his study helps us with two important challenges: to reduce the artificial analytical boundary between the firm and its context, and to move from simple stereotypes to more nuanced characterisations of national and corporate cultures. This book is thoughtful, insightful and unashamedly personal. In keeping with the opening quote of the book by Edward T. Hall the reader comes away with a strong sense that the author has learnt more about his own culture through his reflections about others.'

— Simon Collinson, *Professor of International Business and Innovation, Dean, Birmingham Business School, University of Birmingham, UK*

Routledge Frontiers of Business Management

For a full list of titles in this series, please visit www.routledge.com/series/rfbm

Japanese Management

International perspectives

Hitoshi Iwashita

LONDON AND NEW YORK

First published 2017
by Routledge

2 Park Square, Milton Park, Abingdon, Oxfordshire OX14 4RN
711 Third Avenue, New York, NY 10017

Routledge is an imprint of the Taylor & Francis Group, an informa business

First issued in paperback 2018

British Library Cataloguing in Publication Data
A catalogue record for this book is available from the British Library

Library of Congress Cataloging in Publication Data
Names: Iwashita, Hitoshi, 1972– author.
Title: Japanese management : international perspectives / by Hitoshi
    Iwashita.
Description: Abingdon, Oxon ; New York, NY : Routledge, 2017. |
    Series: Routledge frontiers of business management ; 5 | Includes
    bibliographical references and index.
Identifiers: LCCN 2016028530 | ISBN 9781138680661 (hardback) |
    ISBN 9781315308272 (ebook)
Subjects: LCSH: Management—Japan. | International business
    enterprises—Japan. | Corporations, Japanese.
Classification: LCC HD70.J3 I8696 2017 | DDC 658.00952—dc23
LC record available at https://lccn.loc.gov/2016028530

ISBN: 978-1-138-68066-1 (hbk)
ISBN: 978-1-138-31704-8 (pbk)

Typeset in Galliard
by Apex CoVantage, LLC

Contents

Figures

Tables

Preface

Culture hides more than it reveals, and strangely enough what it hides, it hides most effectively from its participants. Years of study have convinced me that the real job is not to understand foreign culture, but to understand our own.

(Hall, 1973, p. 29)

Before I started this research project, I had been an independent management consultant for large Japanese multinational corporations. I thought that I understood how Japanese multinationals managed their locals in cross-cultural environments. Through my consulting services, recurrent issues on managers in Japanese multinationals appeared to be almost universal. They have issues relating to the differences in languages, perspectives, ways of management and styles of decision making with the locals. In the beginning, I thought of myself as Westernised in terms of knowledge and experience. This view was both right and wrong. I found that I am Westernised when informants talk about their view of 'company as family', but not when talking about their biological Japanese 'family' prioritising of the *ko-on* relationship in Japan, or the reciprocal obligation of Japanese children as explained in this book. Through many interviews and observations at the JapanCo group, I came to 'understand my own' culture as Hall said, rather than to understand that of Japanese expatriates and local employees.

This book is about the lives of Japanese and local employees in the subsidiaries of a Japanese MNC in the West and Asia. The data was collected through interviews, as well as participant and non-participant observation. The objectives of this project were to interpret how actors make sense of their worlds at a Japanese MNC in the West and in Asia. It is my intention to show how Japanese ways of management are understood not only by the locals but also by the Japanese from a Japanese perspective. During data collection, I was not a stranger to targeted JapanCo group MNC because I had delivered some projects for them through my previous consulting job. I expected that some of the interviewees would request for advice concerning their business, so I gave my advice to them whenever it was requested. This helps address the dynamics and relationality of Japanese management practices in the West and in Asia. The ways of Japanese management are accepted, rejected and modified partially according to their locations.

In writing this book, I have been fortunate to have had the support of many relevant people. I would like to thank to my colleagues at Cardiff Business School. In particular, I am grateful to my PhD supervisors, Professor Hugh Willmott and Reader Tim Edwards, for their guidance and support. Many thanks to all of the informants for their time and for allowing me to access to all of the resources. Within my family, my thanks and love to my parents, Mitsugu and Yoko. Most importantly, the biggest thank you to my father, Mitsugu, who has unintentionally continued to invite me to this type of study through my childhood and his understanding during the time of my PhD and writing this book.

1 Introduction

1.1 Introduction

> Is this [subsidiary] a Japanese company?

During interviews, I have often asked this question of both local employees as well as Japanese expatriates in their subsidiaries in Asia and the West of a Japanese multinational company, known here by the alias 'JapanCo'. Responses to this question varied according to different reasons. In Thailand, a Thai manager quickly responded with a big smile to this question by saying, 'yes'. He then described his intimate relationships with his subordinates as 'we are 'family'. They went out for dinner a few times per week. The manager was familiar not only with the professional issues but also the personal lives of his team members. He was confident that he played the role of a 'father' by treating his subordinates as his 'children', in his words. By contrast, in the United States, an American director simply replied, 'Oh boy! It is an American company' in explaining his way of doing business with American customers in the United States. His boss, a president, is an American and the majority of customers are also American, in contrast to Japanese presidents in Asia. This difference illuminates the variations within a Japanese MNC. On closer look, this variation is not limited to the subsidiaries in each geographical location in Asia and the West. It exists even within the subsidiaries according to the Japanese expatriates and local employees in their organisational contexts.

The idea for this book emerged from my previous professional and personal experiences. It originally dates back to my late teens when I was a high school student in the late 1980s and 'Japanisation' was happening (Oliver and Wilkinson, 1988;1992). My father was a management consultant and educational instructor to Japanese multinational corporations (MNCs) who were entering, or had entered, the US market. At my home in Japan, he often shared his consulting stories about how the United States resisted the Japanese way of management because of cultural differences. In order to manage American employees, he emphasised the significance of teamwork to explain what Japanese management should be like. He asserted that Japanese management is based on the 'family' norm, although I did not understand what that meant at that time. All the stories, as far as I remember, illustrated a vivid contrast of cultural differences:

individualism versus collectivism; professionalism versus paternalism; direct versus indirect communication; personal spaces in communication, etc. These contrasts sounded intellectually interesting to me and posed a question as to what causes these differences. After graduating from university, I worked first in Japanese and then US corporations. Later on, I started to work as an independent management consultant dealing with intercultural issues in organisational development, and this motivated me to return again to this question, which I realised still remained unanswered. Since then, I have decided to pursue this interest further in order to understand the differences between Japanese and Western management more fully.

This book deals with those unanswered questions that were on my mind. It extends the understanding of the constellations of logics in Japanese management practices in Asia and the West (Goodrick and Reay, 2011; Thornton et al., 2012). By adopting comparative ethnographic case studies, it explores the cultural meanings of family, corporation, market and religion at each site of the subsidiaries of JapanCo: Thailand, Taiwan, Belgium and the United States. In so doing, the book addresses a new cultural space in an institutional logic approach (Thornton et al., 2012) in the sense that the constellations of logics in Asia are to some extent different from those in the West. Here, Asia primarily means Southeast Asia and North Asia, such as Taiwan, Thailand, Korea and Japan. The West mainly refers to Western Europe and North America, such as the United Kingdom, the United States and Belgium.

1.2 Audience of the book

There are three main audiences for this book. The first audience are institutionalists who theorise and examine institutional logics. Members of this group include Elizabeth Goodrick and Trish Reay, who developed constellations of logics (Goodrick and Reay, 2011; Waldorff, Reay, and Goodrick, 2013); Patricia H Thornton and her colleagues, who presented institutional logic perspectives (Thornton et al., 2012); Royston Greenwood and his colleagues, who raised institutional complexity (Greenwood et al., 2011); Friedland and colleagues, who coined and continued to develop institutional logics (Friedland and Alford, 1991; Friedland et al., 2014); and Rick Delbridge and Tim Edwards, who proposed relational analysis (Delbridge and Edwards, 2007; 2013). The second audience are Japanese management scholars who investigate Japanese management practices. This group includes Nick Oliver and Barry Wilkinson, who elaborated on Japanisation (Oliver and Wilkinson, 1988, 1992); Tony Elger and Chris Smith, who criticised Japanisation (Elger and Smith, 1994, 2005); Dorinne K. Kondo, who elaborated on 'company as family' in a small Japanese firm in Japan (Kondo, 1990); and Anita D. Bhappu, who proposed the existence of 'family' logic in Japanese MNCs (Bhappu, 2000). The third audience includes business managers who work with Japanese MNCs. These managers can be either Japanese or non-Japanese.

1.3 Structure of the book

Chapter 2 identifies gaps in current research and specify the research questions these gaps pose by reviewing the existing literature on Japanese management practices. The practices reviewed are non-manufacturing as well as manufacturing practices identified with Japan. These practices are Total Quality Management (TQM), Quality Control Circle (QC Circle), Just In Time (JIT), lifetime employment and seniority-based wages (Oliver and Wilkinson, 1988; 1992; Ackroyd et al., 1988). Here, the initial argument was whether manufacturing practices can be transferred to Western regions as 'best practice'. Later, this universal model of best practice began to attract heavy criticism centred on a lack consideration for different geographical contexts such as social and economic conditions (Elger and Smith, 1994; 2005). A series of unsuccessful transfers of manufacturing practices led to 'hybrids' of Japanese and non-Japanese management practices (Elger and Smith, 2005).

Nonetheless, this strong emphasis on transferring practices overlooked another important aspect of the practice embodying cultural meanings such as the 'company as family' and employees as 'family' members (Kondo, 1990). In respect to the concept of the company as family, workers in Japanese MNCs are considered to be reciprocal family members who share collective responsibility and identities. In this way, organisational harmony, a striving for consensus, seniority and slow promotion in exchange for a lifetime's employment are prioritised (e.g. Hatvany and Pucik, 1981; Keys and Miller, 1984). In light of this review, four research gaps within Japanese MNC subsidiaries have been identified:

- Few in-depth comparative case studies of Japanese MNCs have been conducted spanning Asia and the West.
- Little attention has been paid to the cultural meanings attributed to practices.
- The manner in which Japanese expatriates and local employees are organised has had little scrutiny.

Hence, drawing on these research gaps, three research questions have been defined regarding Japanese MNC sales subsidiaries:

1 Does the focus on the subsidiaries of a Japanese MNC help to illuminate how practices are being conducted across Asia and the West?
2 Does the focus on the subsidiaries of a Japanese MNC help to illuminate how different cultural meanings are being attributed to practices across Asia and the West?
3 Does the focus on the subsidiaries of a Japanese MNC help to illuminate how Japanese expatriates and local employees are being organised?

Japanese MNCs across borders are expected to generate hybrids (Elger and Smith, 2005; Endo et al., 2015). These hybrids and changes can only be interpreted through attributing meanings in practices across Asia and the West. Drawing on Abo (2015), Asia is defined as primarily Southeast Asian countries and East Asian such as South Korea, Taiwan and China, while the West means Western European and North American countries such as the United Kingdom, Belgium and the United States. The institutional logic approach offers a way of focusing on the variety of meanings attributed by such practices to illuminate how meanings are culturally and institutionally attached to Japanese management practices across Asia and the West.

Chapter 3 formulates a conceptual framework to analyse practices across the subsidiaries of a Japanese MNC. It builds on the current literature on institutional logic (Thornton et al., 2012) and constellations of logics (Goodrick and Reay, 2011), and applies the insights to different geographical contexts in which the Japanese MNC's subsidiaries operate. Constellations of logics are composed of cooperative as well as competitive relationships among logics, possibly illuminating the complicated processes involved in a Japanese MNC. Furthermore, given the constellations of logics, the family, corporation, market and religion are identified and elaborated. In particular, non-market logics such as family and religion are identified as areas of focus. Family logic is rooted in Japanese society where Japanese management practices are born and inculcated. Family logic in Japanese management does not depend on whether a company is owned by a family. Rather, it operates among the interpersonal relationships between management and employees as the Japanese reciprocal relationship based on *ko* and *on* (returning favours to one's parents) within a firm, characterising 'company as family' (Kondo, 1990). Lifetime employment, teamwork and consensus orientation are closely associated with family logic. The chapter also examines other religions, markets and corporation logics. These logics are targeted to characterise and interpret practices in a Japanese MNC. They are deeply rooted in geographical communities in the subsidiaries of Japanese MNCs. Their relationships can be different in Asia and the West.

Chapter 4 identifies the research design and justifies the research methods in order to answer the research questions. 'Practice theory' (Giddens, 1984) is combined with an institutional logic approach, subsuming all the levels of analysis, such as individuals, organisations and society (Friedland and Alford, 1991) into a comprehensive concept of 'practices' as an 'ongoing series of practical activities (Giddens, 1976, p. 81)'. The purpose of the research is to understand the cultural meanings of practices through the constellations of logics. A comparative ethnographic case study is selected as the main type of research. It is comparative across not only Asia but also the West, where constellations of logics were originally identified and theorised. It is ethnographic because 'at home ethnography' is adopted. It is important to have 'natural access' to the research target, a Japanese MNC, rather than as 'a professional stranger'. Through my natural settings, I selected JapanCo as a case. I have long known the Japanese MNC as my father's client. Some of the interviewees have known me since I was young, although I did not necessarily remember them. Data collection and analysis are organised based on 'at home ethnography' (Alvesson, 2009). Thus, the interpretation of data starts from the beginning of data collection and finishes only at the end of the writing process. Through the iterative process of interpretation, self-reflexivity is promoted and utilised. I examined and interacted with the meanings of the topic not as 'a neutral data collector' but as an 'active and reflective' agent (Mason, 2002).

Chapter 5 provides relevant background for interpreting the remaining empirical chapters. With the alliance partner AmericaCo, JapanCo is characterised as a unique and atypical Japanese corporation, possibly causing complex cultural meanings in practices through varied constellations of logics. Here, two major elements influencing the cultural interpretations of each subsidiary in terms of collective identities are provided: the main type of local customers and the dependence on JHQ. Identified as 'a typical Japanese company', JapanCo Thailand (JTHAI) seems to be associated with Japanese management practices and has a large Japanese customer base. By contrast, JapanCo USA (JUSA) and JapanCo EU (JEU) are strongly influenced by AmericaCo and their local customers, thereby being identified as 'an American company' and a mixture of a 'Japanese and a European company' by their local employees. JTAIW is facing a change in its customer base from Japanese to non-Japanese, such as Taiwanese and Chinese, yet being identified as 'a Japanese company'. Furthermore, an examination was also made of the dependence on the resources of JHQ where research and development functions are concentrated. In particular, JUSA is relatively independent from JHQ because of their manufacturing and research and development (R&D) functions, while the others, such as JTHAI, JapanCo Taiwan (JTAIW) and JEU, rely on manufacturing and R&D resources from JHQ. These subsidiaries have to communicate frequently with JHQ to enquire about and negotiate prices, delivery and product quality.

Chapter 6 explores how the practices of customer development are culturally interpreted through cooperative relationships between logics. Targeted practices are study groups, on-the-job training and sales follow-up. Two main findings are identified in this chapter. First, Japanese 'family' and Thai Theravada Buddhism logics are culturally interpreted according to their national cultures. The Japanese family is governed by reciprocal *ko* and *on* relationships, rather than the 'unconditional loyalty' that legitimates the Western family (Thornton et al., 2012). *Oyabun kobun* and *Senpai* are expressed as a burden of Japanese family members: *Ongaeshi* is repayment to whomever one owes a debt, especially in the context of a child or subordinate obligated to return a favour to parents or seniors for the nurturing they offered. Furthermore, the Thai Theravada Buddhism logic is also culturally interpreted and differently enacted. Both Japanese family and Thai Theravada Buddhism once again highlight the limitations of the current Western institutional logics perspective, eventually implying that these perspectives cannot be universally applied. Second, culturally enacted logics can be amplified in a cooperative manner. This finding directly elaborates on the presupposition of amplification itself (Greenwood et al., 2010; 2011).

Chapter 7 explores how work and employment practices are interpreted through contextually competitive relationships among logics that may coexist and in turn conflict. Targeted practices are job delegation, performance appraisal and socialisation. The main finding of this chapter is that the constellations of logics are ongoing and continuously formed in relation to geographical locations because contextually enacted logics do not necessarily 'win' or 'lose' for lengthy periods of time in practice. Although there are means to deal with and finally resolve the competitive relationships – e.g. 'actors' active collaboration' (Reay and Hinnings, 2005; 2009), 'compartmentalisation' (Greenwood et al., 2011) – these are not adopted here to mediate the competitive relationship. Rather, negotiation and conflict continue to be played out by actors on an ongoing basis. This situation further negates the concept of one-off 'segmenting', which aims to separate the impacts of logics on different actors, geographical communities and organisations once and for all to solve the conflicts caused by competitive relationships (Goodrick and Reay, 2011). Moreover, the constellations of logics are, to some extent, different in Asia and the West, which elaborates on the geographical communities in which specific logics are rooted (Marquis and Lounsbury, 2007; Lounsbury, 2007). In Asia, the family logic is enacted through the practices of employment. By contrast, in the West, market logic is strongly enacted by performance appraisal and socialisation (see 7.3.1). As Abo (2015) and Lounsbury (2007) point out, geographical location matters. However, the geographical locations in Asia and the West do not automatically determine the competitive relationships between logics.

Chapter 8 explores how the practices in work organisations are interpreted through ceremonial aspects and how actors in turn are organised. It also corresponds primarily, but not exclusively, to the third research question of how Japanese and locals are organised. Targeted practices are communication with JHQ about the performance evaluation of Japanese expatriates, business results and complaints of the locals. The main finding of this chapter is that the boundaries of organisational communities are not 'segmented' to Japanese expatriates but constructed through actors' profiles. The finding further elaborates on the receptivity of 'intraorganisational communities', which is supposed to affect the given meaning of logics in the subsidiaries. Greenwood et al. (2011) argue that receptivity may be strongly affected by 'the thickness of ties' of organisational communities to their organisational fields. At first sight, these thick ties seem to support Japanese organisational communities. Japanese expatriates are structured as the dominant organisational community, manifesting *uchi*, or the inside group of the ethnocentric family (Kondo, 1990). The boundaries of these organisational communities are not prefixed, however, but contested and dynamically redrawn in relation to the actors' personal profiles. Here, the boundaries are occasionally contested by examining who becomes family members through their 'active participation'. Moreover, the receptivity of Japanese organisational communities is greatly affected by actors' profiles, as is strongly implied by Suddaby et al. (2012) and Battilana and Dorado (2010). This tendency indicates that the organisational communities are constructed through actors' 'life history' in terms of logics, as Battilana and Dorado (2010) imply, rather than by the organisational field structures (Greenwood et al., 2011).

Chapter 9 summarises the key findings, their significance, the implications for managers and limitations and future questions. The four main findings are located in the constellations of logics. First, the finding that the cooperative relationships between family and religion logics are culturally embodied by the practices in customer development highlights the serious limitations of the institutional logic approach, which is based on Western society (Thornton et al., 2012). Second, the finding that both Japanese family and Theravada Buddhism are strengthening each other directly supports the presupposition of amplification itself (Greenwood et al., 2010; 2011), while elaborating the facilitative relationship among logics which simply guides practices without conflict (Goodrick and Reay, 2011). Third, the finding that the constellations of logics are ongoing and continuously formed in relation to geographical locations contrasts with the institutionalists' strong focus on static competition between two logics such as 'segmenting' (Goodrick and Reay, 2011) or 'compartmentalisation' (Greenwood et al., 2011). Fourth, the finding that the boundaries of organisational communities are not 'segmented' to Japanese expatriates but constructed through actors' profiles raises the importance of an actor's profile and supports the possible institutional reflexivity of actors, as Suddaby et al. (2012) point out.

2 Company as family in Japanese MNCs?

2.1 Introduction

This chapter identifies the research gaps and their accompanying questions by reviewing the existing literature on Japanese management practices, meaning the practices identified with Japan. It is divided into five sections. First, the chapter reviews the practices at Japanese manufacturing plants. Second, it elaborates on the cultural meaning of 'company as family'. Third, it explores the cultural meanings for practices considered different between Asian and Western regions. Fourth, a concluding section summarises the research gaps based on existing literature and ultimately determines the research questions to be answered. Finally, I provide personal reflection on the meanings of 'Japanese family'.

2.2 Japanisation as a diffusion of Japanese management practices

First, let's look at the historical development of Japanisation. The concept of Japanisation emerged with the growing interest in competitive Japanese corporations (e.g. Pascal and Athos, 1982; Schonberger, 1982). Since the 1970s, Japan's economic success led management scholars to examine the practices of major corporations; an increasing interest in Japanese firms and Japan stems from its economic growth until the 1980s. The study of Japanese firms was clearly a hot topic at that time, when Vogel (1979) identified Japan as the 'number one' economy in the world, and as a lesson for Americans. In this era, the situation in Japan was an exciting topic, and the manufacturing practices identified with Japan were seen as 'best practice' as well as a source of a firm's competitive advantage (Oliver and Wilkinson, 1988; 1992). After the economic bubble burst in the 1990s, however, these practices were seriously questioned and criticised.

2.2.1 Japanisation with the success of the Japanese economy during the 1980s

With a strong emphasis on manufacturing practices, Peter Turnbull (1986) analysed how a Western company in the United Kingdom, the component supplier Lucas Electrical, adopted the manufacturing methods used by large Japanese companies, these being methods such as Just In Time (JIT) and Quality Control Circle (QC Circle). Using a case study method, he chronologically analysed the entire process, from the introduction of these production techniques to the organisational arrangement for developing these methods. Following this analysis, Oliver and Wilkinson (1988; 1992) published *The Japanization of British Industry*, identifying and measuring the diffusion of Japanese management practices and culture in Western countries. Here, they defined Japanisation as:

> An umbrella term to refer to the process by which some aspects of UK industry appeared to be converging towards a Japanese-style model of management practice. This process encompassed two strands – the emulation of Japanese manufacturing methods by Western manufacturers and also the increasing volume of Japanese direct manufacturing investment in Western economies.
>
> (Oliver and Wilkinson, 1988, p. 1)

Both practices of convergence and direct investment went hand-in-hand in the United Kingdom, in the sense that both of them could be causes and effects. This view extended the concept of Japanisation in relation to personnel practices and business policy in social and economic contexts. In addition to carrying out a survey, they adopted case studies of Japanese and British manufacturers in the United Kingdom focusing primarily on production techniques, in particular, Just-In-Time (JIT), and secondarily on personnel practices, labour policy and even work organisation. The motivation for adopting these practices was to acquire the same competitive advantage achieved by Japanese MNCs.

Oliver and Wilkinson (1988) demonstrated the interdependencies between each practice and the external environment. Manufacturing practices such as JIT and TQM demand teamwork and cooperation, with a commitment from employees in exchange for seniority and lifetime employment (where their jobs are secured until retirement age). Moreover, these interdependencies went hand-in-hand with cooperative relations between buyers and suppliers, with finance institutions, trade unions and workers. Thus, the manufacturing practices are not stand-alone but are dependent on other practices and particular social, economic and political conditions, these being similar to those of Japanese society. These supportive conditions, for example, could be a labour surplus of young workers, a new manufacturing site welcoming recent practices, stable industrial relations, cooperative workers and trade unions, all supporting a set of 'Japanese style industrial organisation'. This study, therefore, brilliantly succeeded in presenting a snapshot of what was happening in the manufacturing plants in the United Kingdom.

Making a comparison with the data presented in the first edition of their book in 1988 with their second edition, Oliver and Wilkinson (1992) indicated the relatively unsuccessful results of adopting Japanese manufacturing practices in

1991. This outcome demonstrates the 'obstacles to Japanisation' in the United Kingdom, indicating that this approach could be 'culturally embedded' in Japan. For example, one obstacle referred to as 'the paternalism of the personnel practices' entails 'the dilution of occupation-specific expertise and the salience of internal promotion (p. 328)', thereby denying individual rights and mobility of the workers. Another obstacle is the long-term relationship between buyers and suppliers that eventually leads to large corporations passing on 'the cost of holding inventories' to the suppliers. They also exert control over the trade unions inside the supply companies, thereby reducing the autonomy of the suppliers. A further example of an obstacle is that of a collaborative, single, strike-free, enterprise trade union that coexists with company advisory boards. This group consists of union and non-union members, thereby contradicting the adversarial role of a trade union based on industry and occupations. In addition, Japanese banks, which provide 'low-interest' and 'long-term loans', contrast with British banks that are oriented to 'a short term profit mentality' based on the stock market in the United Kingdom. Notwithstanding, Oliver and Wilkinson (1992) concluded that these obstacles could be overcome by establishing 'functional equivalents' to the conditions found in Japan. For example, workers could be trained to be familiar with paternalism while trade unions could be managed by setting up a company advisory board.

Ackroyd et al. (1988) in 'The Japanisation of British industry?' also observed these interdependencies among manufacturing practices, as well as their external conditions, but reached a different conclusion. This study offered a critique of the term 'Japanisation' as a homogenous phenomenon, by comparing and contrasting the different socio-economic systems of Britain and Japan. Bearing in mind the societal and economic environment, they examined the concept of Japanisation from shop-floor practices to institutional contexts, examining areas such as the employment system, the labour market, finance and investment policy. They also pointed out how social and economic conditions in Britain are distinctively different from those of Japan. This difference occurs because conditions in Britain involve a 'lack of integration' between finance institutions and manufacturers, have 'highly fragmented' capital in the global economy, are not manufacturers and there is no state intervention to manage demand rather than orchestrate industrial development (Ackroyd et al., 1988). Thus, they concluded that the success of Japanisation was embedded within a society in which a set of social and economic relations supports its preferable conditions; this underlines the dangers inherent in transferring Japanese management practices.

2.2.2 Critiques of Japanisation after the bubble economy in the early 1990s

At the beginning of the 1990s when the Japanese bubble economy burst, the Japanese economy started to decline and had minimal growth (Keizer, 2012). In line with this economic stagnation, Elger and Smith (1994) published a book entitled *Global Japanization?*, which seriously questioned the optimistic assumptions of

Oliver and Wilkinson (1988; 1992) that Japanese management practices could be transferable as best practice across different geographical contexts. Their work provides a series of unsuccessful cases where the manufacturing practices of Japanese and non-Japanese corporations were transferred to North America, Europe and Latin America. In regard to Subaru-Isuzu Automotive (SIA) in the United States, Graham (1994) described the American workers' resistance to Japanese corporation rituals such as 'morning exercises, team meetings, department meetings and company celebrations'. Here, collective and individual forms of resistance to the rituals emerged in various forms: a refusal to do exercise, anonymous letters, conflict over shift rotations and leaving a moving assembly line.

In terms of the Canadian Automotive Manufacturing Inc. (CAMI), 'a unionized joint venture automobile assembly plant' in Canada, Rinehart et al. (1994) found that Canadian workers were barely motivated to participate in Japanese manufacturing practices, such as continuous improvement and the suggestion programmes, eventually characterising them as 'a polite way to get more out of us'. Given these unsuccessful cases in a concrete setting, it is perhaps not surprising that Elger and Smith (1994) raised serious doubts about the transferability of Japanese management practices as innovative best practices. In their study, they identified a Japanese corporation as a 'transplant'; a mechanism in which Japanese management practices (primarily manufacturing practices but also personnel) could be transferred to different geographical locations, except in Japan.

Later on, Elger and Smith (2005) published a study entitled 'Assembly work', characterising the practices in Japanese MNCs as 'hybrids', thereby reflecting societal effects in both the home and host countries, such as 'different national institutions, cultures, and histories' (p. 58). Conducting five case studies of Japanese MNCs in the United Kingdom, Elger and Smith (2005) examined how Japanese MNC plants in the United Kingdom operate differently in terms of the policies and practices surrounding a manufacturing function. These policies and practices can be seen in *nemawashi* ('consensus orientation'), *ho-ren-so* ('information sharing'), lifetime or long-term employment, seniority and on-the-job training. However, these practices may be applied differently because a manufacturing plant can be 'a strong mediator of both home and host countries effects (p. 365)'. This makes it possible to view these effects differently according to each plant, each in a different company network of suppliers, customers and with their own headquarters. On the one hand, a large plant might draw on best practices within its parent company and sister plants, while on the other hand, a small plant might have a limited-sized network and thus experience greater influence from its customers. In this way, the effects of home and host countries on manufacturing practices are mediated by each plant in a given location, its relationship to other subsidiaries and its parent companies.

2.2.3 Organising Japanese expatriates and local employees

With the critiques of Japanisation, we can discuss the work organisation dominated by Japanese expatriates. Here, the work organisation within the subsidiaries of Japanese MNCs is divided between Japanese expatriates and local employees when communicating with external organisations, such as with the headquarters and local customers. Elger and Smith (2005) characterised these divides as the two management structures of the Japanese and locals. Although they did not elaborate on this structural divide or attribute the meanings of the 'family', their interview data is consistent with this division between the Japanese and locals. In their comparative case studies of Japanese plants in the United Kingdom, two management structures were identified: one is a Japanese management structure while the other is British management structure. The Japanese management structure promotes teamwork and a high commitment from workers, while the British have a more direct approach to the local workforce, by using command and control. The Japanese believed that British managers did not make enough effort to implement Japanese management practices. On the other hand, British managers were sceptical about the effects of these practices, and considered that the Japanese did not share enough information, given the fact that they were limited in participating in the decision-making process. This divide clearly indicates that the cultural meanings of family may be confined to the groups of Japanese expatriates, leading them to treat British managers as outsiders.

Similarly, Kopp (1999, p. 122) described two management structures as a 'vicious circle of lack of trust'. Using a survey and a case study, she attributes this type of divide between the Japanese and Americans to the Japanese language barrier, indirect communication, consensus-oriented decision making, slow promotion and lifetime employment. Here, possible divisions emerge between Japanese and Americans: Japanese managers may state, 'We don't want to give too much information and responsibility to locally hired employees right away, because they might job-hop to another company (ibid).' When this occurs, local employees may feel excluded from the decision-making process and conclude that their future with the company is limited, and then leave to join another company. At this point, Japanese managers might say, 'Ah, it's just what we thought, non-Japanese aren't loyal to their companies. They didn't stick around enough for us to get to trust them! (ibid).' Given these cases, she concludes that this 'vicious circle of lack of trust' represents the exportation of the two-tier Human Resources Management (HRM) system in Japan between *seishain* and non-*seishain*, or 'core' and 'peripheral' Japanese employees. In Japan, core employees in a permanent contract are expected to receive long-term benefits, such as lifetime and long-term employment, seniority-based compensation and high investment in training. By contrast, peripheral employees on temporary contracts gain few benefits. In practice, there are highly likely to be two different management structures for Japanese and locals.

These two management structures have become obvious. Initially, Westney (1987; 1999) indicated the importance of Japanese expatriates when operating Japanese MNC subsidiaries, which was based on the need to communicate with headquarters. In particular, Japanese expatriates were expected to play a central role in transferring and controlling manufacturing methods from the headquarters in Japan. Kopp (1999), for example, described how Japanese expatriates dominate the decision-making process, not local employees or management. A study concerning the subsidiaries of Japanese MNCs in Europe and the United States showed that local managers were involved in less than half the decisions concerning local business, according to Beechler et al. (1996). These decisions were made only by Japanese expatriates or at the headquarters in Japan.

The dominance of Japanese expatriates has had a considerable influence in generating an ethnocentric Japanese culture in the subsidiaries of Japanese MNCs (see 8.2). The typical work organisation at Japanese plants is one where a Japanese expatriate is assigned as an 'advisor' in the margin of an organisational chart (Elger and Smith, 2005). A Japanese expatriate manager is expected to support and advise a line manager by closely working with his or her workers. Westney (1999, p. 26) summarised this structure as follows: 'Since the very earliest stages of internationalization, Japanese MNCs have been criticised for their heavy reliance on expatriate middle-level managers to act as the key cross-border integrators.' This dominance was also investigated in comparison with Western MNCs focusing on the formal control of their subsidiaries. Ferner (1997) offers a vivid account of the unique features of Japanese expatriates. He describes the Japanese approach as 'strong but informal centralised co-ordination of foreign operations, highly reliant on establishing an international network of Japanese expatriate managers' (Ferner, 1997, p. 21–22). This case seems to be true in some Japanese MNCs (Elger and Smith, 2005), perhaps generating ceremonial aspects within the work organisation.

Given these two structures within the subsidiaries, the cultural meanings of the 'family' might be restricted and contested within Japanese communities or across certain groups or units, although group orientation may not be the correct term for expressing a feature of the Japanese family. Kondo (1990) points out that there is no sense of individualism in the Japanese family because '[b]y speaking, one inevitably speaks as a person embedded within a particular *uchi*. One is never an isolated individual (Kondo, 1990, p. 147).' In a sense, this cultural boundary of the family is considered to be different between Asian and the Western regions, as well as in the ways the subsidiaries communicate with headquarters. In Asia, the cultural meanings of the family might be accepted and interpreted, even outside of Japanese expatriate groups. In the West, however, they may be restricted to only Japanese expatriate groups. Alternatively, it might not exist anymore due to the recent changes in Japanese management practices (Keizer, 2012). The next subsection examines the cultural meaning of the family in Japanese society.

2.3 'Company as family' in Japanese management practices

Japanese management practices do not stand alone in Japanese society and culture (e.g. Turnbull, 1986): they need to be considered with regard to their characteristics through 'area knowledge' of its culture and language (Elger and Smith, 2005). In fact, some scholars have touched on the strong association of Japanese management practices with the 'family' norm in Japanese society (e.g. Hartvany and Pucik, 1981; Keys and Miller, 1984). Japanese paternalism is expected to exist behind Japanese management practices in the same way as organisational members treat corporations as a family or community, sharing 'a common destiny'. This kinship relationship is apparent in the practices of JIT, TQM, and QC circles, enabling organisational members to work as a team, and ultimately as a 'family', with a particular job security, such as lifetime employment. This relationship is also likely to be the case in groups of corporations, such as *keiretsu* ('conglomerates').

2.3.1 Interpreting the meaning of a 'company as family' culturally

The term 'company as family' was used to characterise Japanese MNCs (e.g. Hartvany and Pucik, 1981; Keys and Miller, 1984). Here, the meaning of 'family' in a Japanese MNC has been historically embedded in Japanese society. In the feudal era of the Tokugawa regime from the seventeenth to nineteenth centuries, Bhappu (2000) sees Japanese paternalism behind inter-organisational practices, such as with *keiretsu*, which she argues were close to the structure of ranking in the previous era in Japan. She also asserts that merchants, such as those in feudal households in the Tokugawa regime, also resembled current Japanese corporations:

> Merchant households frequently established *bunke* (branch) *ie* beside the *honke* (main) *ie*. This enabled them to expand their distribution channels geographically. It also provided a way for the "corporate" merchant *ie* to perpetuate itself as an entity from one generation to another.
>
> (p. 411)

Assuming company as family, group orientation, cooperation and *wa* ('harmony') are enhanced and can be institutionally embedded into Japanese management practices. TQM and JIT are not purely a set of economic activities to boost productivity, but strongly embody these cultural meanings of a family among workers. Therefore, it follows that without the norm of family, these practices are unlikely to be adopted and accepted by local workers, as Abo (2015) strongly indicates.

Kondo (1990) explores the contested meanings of a company as family in greater detail. By adopting an ethnographic approach as an active participant in a small Japanese family firm factory in Japan – the Sato company – she reveals how the concepts of company and family are inseparable and intertwined. She claims that the economic ties in the small firm are far beyond the contractual obligations interpreted in the West, 'entailing intense involvement in group outings, ritual obligations, and strong bonds of loyalty, gratitude, and commitment (p. 198)' among its family and organisational members. Furthermore, she argues for the contested meanings of a 'company as family' that are interpreted according to the actors in their contexts. The term *ie* ('household') is understood not only as a physical building for the family on the basis of blood relations but also as ' "hearth", signifying people who belong to the same domestic group (p. 121)'. She asserts that *ie* in Japan should not be treated just as kinship based on biological blood relations, but is 'best understood as corporate groups that hold property (for example, land, a reputation, and an art or "cultural capital") in perpetuity (p. 122).' It serves as a unit of production, of consumption, and as a religious function such as 'ancestor worship' and forms of social welfare. Here, the notion of family is cultural in the same way that an American family is limited to biological relationships and conjugal ties (Kondo, 1990).

This notion of *ie* and family can also be scrutinised through the Japanese language. *Uchi no kaisha* ('my company') is interpreted, contested and appropriated by actors in a particular context. For employees, it often means company as family by caring family members and reminding those members of the obligation of loyalty. For their managers, however, this notion can be manipulated for economic benefits; Kondo (1990, p. 213) describes the owner's 'family' of the Sato 'awarding low wages, berating them unjustly, conducting sporadic surveillance of shop-floor activities'. In particular, the workers may start to criticise the owner who is 'inadequately familial' if the owner emphasises the economic rationality of the company by pursing economic efficiency that is not right for the 'company as family'. In terms of an artisan's identity, the workers may criticise their company while often being proud of being members of that company. She demonstrates how the meanings of a company as family can never be coherent or consistent, and have complexities with 'contradictions, nuances, and multiplicities engendered by any act or appropriation of meanings' (p. 218). These nuanced cultural meanings of family have also been identified in large Japanese MNCs (e.g. Hartvany and Pucik, 1981; Keys and Miller, 1984) although they were not fully elaborated on as in the work of Kondo (1990).

Such notions of family, while often contested and appropriated, loosely underpin Japanese management practices, such as TQM and JIT, which require the workers' participation and long hours on the shop floor as family members (Keys and Millar, 1984). This cultural meaning of family is specific to Japan, because the prosperity of families is more significant than of individuals. Keys and Miller (1984, p. 347–8) explain that for the Japanese this means that 'the company becomes a surrogate for the family, work takes on the same ethos as a contribution to the family – loyalty, sincerity . . . the company's (family's) prosperity becomes more important than individual prosperity, and work for the company – not leisure – becomes the essence of life'. This cultural meaning of family constitutes Japanese management practices, and there is an assumption that all the members are obliged to contribute to family prosperity, with this expectation taking precedence over individual needs. This cultural meaning of family explains why shop-floor workers are expected to work long hours and be non-resistant in Japan, as Williams et al. (1994, p. 86) point out, since 'Japanese management in the press shop is technically superior but in many ways socially inferior to Western practices'.

2.3.2 *Resistance to the cultural meanings of 'family'?*

On reflection, the contested meanings of 'company as family' can be considered as an obstacle to the smooth transference of Japanese management practices to the foreign subsidiaries of Japanese MNCs. Graham (1994), for instance, demonstrated the resistance of American local workers at a Japanese MNC plant, thereby presenting a critique of the simple articulation of Japanisation. Adopting an ethnographic approach on the shop floor of Subaru-Isuzu Automotive (SIA) in the United States, and as an employee there, he observed direct confrontation in the form of collective resistance and veiled protest through individual resistance. Here, direct confrontation concerned 'leaving a moving line' and a 'refusal to work', while a veiled protest involved 'anonymous letters', a 'refusal to exercise' and to practice company's rituals, such as 'morning exercises, team meetings, department meetings, and company celebrations'. Although Graham (1994) did not touch upon the cultural meanings of such forms of resistance, the acts of resistance constitute a refusal to attribute Japanese cultural meanings, paternalism and family to the practices. Such rituals are profoundly connected to paternalism in Japanese society and culture, where workers are cooperative and loyal to their corporation through the expression of family. This collective effort expected resistance from American workers who prioritise individuals over organisations. This cultural conflict, albeit not elaborating on cultural meanings in depth, meant that that SIA did not successfully acquire the Japanese egalitarian culture with the norm of cooperation, as other scholars argued in the era of the coined 'Japanisation' (e.g. Elger and Smith, 1994).

In a similar fashion, Delbridge (1998) conducted an ethnographic study at Japanese manufacturing sites in the United Kingdom by working on the shop floor. As a participant observer, he revealed single-skilled workers and a lack of commitment in contrast to the full commitment from multi-skilled workers discussed in a series of Japanisation literature. Here, he found that there was little commitment or loyalty to organisations from workers, but instead, there was 'the persistence of conflicts between management and labour' (p. 151). As with other scholars, he was interested in how Japanese management practices are conducted and resisted in order to examine the transplants of Japanese MNCs, and, as such, cultural meanings were not his main focus. In fact, in-depth ethnographic research on Japanese MNCs has rarely been conducted, let alone a nuanced consideration of the cultural meanings of practices.

A swathe of the literature aims to examine the transferability of management practices in the subsidiaries of Japanese MNCs, but unlike other studies focusing on the transferability of management practices, the work of Kondo (1990) is unique in the sense that she, as a Japanese American ethnographer, gains and utilises 'area knowledge' (Elger and Smith, 2005) in Japan, such as with Japanese culture and language in depth. The focus on cultural meanings should be transferred to the foreign subsidiaries of contemporary Japanese MNCs in light of the burst bubble economy and economic stagnation of Japan, the so-called lost decade since the 1990s (Keizer, 2012). Here, from the point of view of the cultural meanings of the family, there are likely to be conflicts and contradictions among the attributed meanings in its practice, possibly obstructing the transference of practices and causing further resistance from local workers. There is the possibility that the same practice may embody different cultural meanings for different actors in different locations. The next subsection scrutinises the relationality of transferring these practices between Asia and the West.

2.4 The relationality of transferring practices between Asia and the West

The success of transferring Japanese management practices may rest not only on the social and economic conditions of a home country, but also on the culture, values and practices shaped by the conditions of the host country. Abo (2015) argues for differences between regions when transferring practices at Japanese MNCs, bringing their relationality in Asia and the West.

2.4.1 Problems with transferring practices across different geographical locations

Originally, when considering the concept of Japanisation, Turnbull (1986) posed a question about the feasibility of transferring practices into a different geographical location. These practices were built and maintained with 'high-trust' management in Japan, these being developed by coercive elements of Japanese society, but it was possible that they might not work elsewhere. He indicates how

> the introduction of "high-trust" management techniques into essentially "low-trust" environments, where management has traditionally attempted to reduce employee autonomy, discretion and influence through "Taylorist" techniques, is unlikely to foster employee commitment towards managerial objectives.
>
> (p. 203–4)

This raises the question of whether practices can be transferred to different contexts. In fact, this relationality where social and economic contexts in a host country affect transferring practices was later picked up on by Japanese management scholars (e.g. Ackroyd et al., 1988). Here, the idea of relationality is strongly conveyed in the sense that when in a geographical context, such as the high trust between managers and those being managed, supports the implementation of practices, the practices can be easily accepted. When, there is low trust, however, it becomes harder to transfer the practices.

More recently, Abo (2015) indicated the relationality of transferring Japanese management practices between Asia and the West. Based on his research since the 1980s into the implementation of Japanese management methods across six continents, Abo (2015) asserts that Japanese management methods are influenced by the host society and its culture in each region. Although he does not examine culturally embodied meanings in management practices, he points out that a 'group consciousness', such as collectivism and cooperation in a geographical location, does matter in terms of transferring practices. In Abo's research, a high group consciousness identified with Asian countries correlates to the success of Japanese management practice implementation in Asia.

Clearly, the different geographical locations are significant when transferring manufacturing methods and practices. Abo's (2015) methods were based on the degree to which Japanese manufacturing techniques can be transferred from the headquarters to subsidiaries, as is the case in Japan. Here, he adopted a quantitative method, a 'five-point grading system', to measure how practices are transferred as with Japan. He set up an analytical model of application and adaptation, showing either that Japanese manufacturing practices were simply applied to a local context or that they were adapted. The model consisted of a '6-goup 23 item hybrid-evaluation'. Here, the six groups constituted the work of organisation and administration, production control, procurement, group consciousness, labour relations and parent-subsidiary relations. According to Abo (2015), these local contexts behind the practices were influenced by each region. Hence, this societal effect varies depending on the region and the geographical location where Japanese MNCs operate.

2.4.2 Cultural and geographic contexts in Asia and the West

There are two important regions where the relationality of transferring Japanese management practices have been examined: Asia and the West. Here, Asia means primarily Southeast Asian countries and East Asian such as South Korea, Taiwan and China, while the West means Western European and North American countries such as the United Kingdom, Belgium and the United States. In the Asian region, Abo (2015) considers that Japanese MNCs are highly likely to 'apply' Japanese management practices to each country as an 'Asian standard'. In particular, group consciousness, or a group orientation over individuals, is relatively higher in Korea and Taiwan than in European countries. Here, it is thought that these practices may have been attributed by the participants to cultural meanings, yet the meanings were not his focus. Although this geographical effect is not straightforward, it tends to be distinctive according to region, as with Asia and non-Asia. In addition, Collinson and Rugman (2008) connect this to the 'relational embeddedness' of Japanese management practices in Asian regions as well as in Japan, but not in Western regions. This embeddedness comes about partly because there is a large customer base for industrial Japanese manufactured goods in the Asian region. This base reflects that many Japanese MNCs have moved their production to the Asian region to benefit from plentiful labour with low wages (Keizer, 2012). This embeddedness also partly arises because there are cultural similarities in Asia, such as with the importance of kinship and collectivism.

In Thailand, for example, Japanese personnel practices, such as the collective orientation of the Japanese and job security, seem to appeal more than Western MNCs (Atmiyanandana and Lawler, 2003). This further confirms a close cultural distance between Japan and other Asian countries in terms of a common collectivism (Hofstede, 2010).

In contrast, in Western regions, mainly in North America and Western Europe, Abo (2015) assumes that Japanese MNCs are relatively unlikely to apply Japanese management practices to each country as they do in the Asian region. Here, when analysing three Japanese as well as one form of European 'press shop performance', Williams et al. (1994) reviewed the necessary conditions for Japanisation to be possible for Western corporations while questioning how far [the West is] from Japan. A high level of employee commitment is associated with the social and institutional context in Japan. Thus, it was concluded that the social and institutional context of Western management is 'very far from Japan', bringing about difficulties when applying Japanese management practices to the Western context. In a sense, Japanese management practices are deeply supported and connected by their surrounding operations. These practices are manifested in aspects such as group consciousness, collectivism, seniority and lifetime or long-term employment. Williams et al. (1994) characterised the high level of commitment as well as the workers' 'consent and conformity' on the Japanese shop floor as being rewarded with lifetime employment. This view reflects a wide 'cultural distance' between Japan and Western countries in terms of the preferred collectivism in Japan as opposed to the individualism of the West (Hofstede, 2010).

When considering the societal and cultural influences on practices, Williams et al. (1994, p. 86) declared that 'Japanese management in the press shop is technically superior but in many ways socially inferior to Western practices'. This result occurs because shop-floor workers are expected to work long hours and be compliant in Japan. In addition, Elger and Smith (2005) illustrate how Japanese production methods in the United Kingdom have not been adopted by shop-floor workers particularly well because of low pay. Similarly, in Germany, Brannen and Salk (2000) bring out how German managers have been frustrated by the consensus orientation of Japanese management, expressing a feeling of powerlessness. This outcome occurs because in Japanese corporate culture, flexible job roles and group orientation are prioritised, while in Germany there is a well-defined job-role and individual orientation. These cultural conflicts with Japanese management practices may support the low transferability of Japanese management practices to Western regions.

The current literature reviewed here, therefore, raises the possibility that Japanese management practices can be conducted and even interpreted differently according to different societies and cultures across geographical locations, especially in Asian and Western regions. Many studies have analysed the degree of productivity between Japanese and local firms, concluding that there is either high or low transferability (e.g. see Oliver and Wilkinson, 1998; 1992). As Abo

(2015) indicates, however, the significance of relationality should again be seriously scrutinised when transferring practices to Asia and Western regions. This review also raises another possibility, namely that the different cultural meanings regarding the same practices, and this relationality, are better explored across different subsidiaries of a single Japanese MNC in Asian and Western regions.

2.5 Conclusion: research gaps and questions

This chapter identified research gaps and questions by reviewing the existing literature on 'Japanese management practices' and the practices identified with Japan. Japanisation was originally treated as a homogeneous phenomenon (Oliver and Wilkinson, 1992) but is now seen as hybrids of Japanese and local management practices in given geographic contexts (Elger and Smith, 2005). Furthermore, Abo's (2015) comparative study on the application and adaptation of Japanese management practices raises the possibility that cultural meanings can be attached to practices differently. Japanese management practices are embedded in Japanese society and culture but are now expected to be adapted to the society and culture where they are conducted.

In the light of this review, three research gaps within Japanese MNCs subsidiaries have been identified:

1 few in-depth comparative case studies have been conducted within Japanese MNCs spanning Asia and the West
2 little attention has been paid to the cultural meanings attributed to the practices
3 the manner in which Japanese expatriates and local employees are organised has been the subject of little scrutiny

First, few in-depth comparative case studies have been conducted within Japanese MNCs (see 2.5). Many studies compare and contrast cases, in the same location, either between Japanese and local corporations or among Japanese corporations. (e.g. Oliver and Wilkinson, 1988; 1992; Elger and Smith, 2005). This practice occurs because Japanese manufacturing plants often tend to be examined to prove the high productivity of their practices in comparison to other local plants. Thus, the units of comparison and contrast tend to be different for local plants in the same geographic context. This difference suggests that in-depth comparative case studies within a single Japanese MNC are required. Nonetheless, in summarising the adoption of manufacturing practices at Japanese MNCs across six continents, the recent review of Abo (2015) demonstrates that there can be a variety of cultural interpretations of transferred manufacturing practices in Asia and the Western regions. In Korea and Taiwan, where there is a relatively high group consciousness among workers, the practices tend to be conducted as they would be in Japan, while in North America and Europe, where there is a low group consciousness among workers, the practices are not well adopted. This result indicates that there are distinctive cultural as well as societal differences between Asia and the West.

Second, the cultural meanings of the 'company as family' attributed to practices are rarely discussed (see 2.3). This lack may possibly explain why a set of transferred Japanese management practices were not easily achieved in the West, as discussed in Japanisation (e.g. Oliver and Wilkinson, 1988; 1992; Elger and Smith, 1994; 2005). The primary focus on the transferability of the material practices does not give much attention to their cultural meanings. In contrast, Kondo (1990) strongly emphasises the embodied cultural meanings through practices and the company as family, which possibly underpins the features of manufacturing practices: group orientation, harmony and cooperation. None-theless, the cultural meanings of the family have been focused on less frequently in the literature. Overall, the current literature suggests that the manufacturing practices at plants have long been the main units of analysis, but that these are distanced from the cultural meanings ascribed to those practices across different geographical locations.

This is understandable since many Japanese management scholars, with the exception of Kondo (1990), a Japanese American, are 'non-Japanese speaking industrial sociologists', and therefore are fundamentally lacking an 'area knowledge of Japan'; this refers to society, national institutions, cultural practices and languages in Japan (Elger and Smith, 2005). Focusing on area knowledge makes it possible to further understand another aspect in the transfer of practices, namely embodied cultural meanings.

Third, little of the literature examines the extent to which Japanese expatriates and local employees are divided into two groups (see 2.3.3). This might be due to cultural differences, as Kopp (1999) discusses, or to some other structural support from the headquarters. Here, she touches on the dominant position of Japanese expatriates assigned by headquarters. The cultural differences among Japanese, Americans and Europeans makes it possible to isolate the Japanese from local employees, but she does not mention in depth what constitutes the management structures across Asian and Western regions. Elger and Smith (2005) simply share the interviewee's comment that there seem to be two management structures between Japanese expatriates and British employees, but do not elaborate on what divides these structures.

These research gaps are consistent with the tendency for Japanese management practices to be researched as macro-level studies with quantitative methods, focusing on the material aspects of transferring practices, rather than their meanings. A considerable amount of the literature, with some exemptions (e.g. Delbridge, 1998), use quantitative methods because interviews in English are considered not to be well understood by Japanese expatriates (Kopp, 1999). Due to the diversity and complexity of practices in Japanese MNCs with different social, institutional and cultural effects, the practices, even if exactly applied as in Japan, may be interpreted differently with different cultural meanings. Hence, drawing on these research gaps, three research questions have been defined regarding Japanese MNC sales subsidiaries:

1   Does the focus on the subsidiaries of a Japanese MNC help to illuminate how practices are being conducted across Asia and the West?
2   Does the focus on the subsidiaries of a Japanese MNC help to illuminate how cultural meanings are being attributed differently to non-manufacturing practices across Asia and the West?
3   Does the focus on the subsidiaries of a Japanese MNC help to illuminate ow Japanese expatriates and local employees are being organised?

Japanese MNCs across borders are expected to generate hybrids (Elger and Smith, 2005; Endo et al., 2015). These hybrids and changes can only be interpreted through attributed meanings in practices across different geographic contexts. A variety of meanings attributed by such practices can be focused on by adopting the recently developed institutional logic approach to illuminate how meanings are culturally and institutionally attached to Japanese management practices across borders. Chapter 2 introduces the institutional logic approach and discusses it as a conceptual framework to further explore this question.

2.6   Personal reflection: my experience working at a Japanese corporation

'Company as family' may sound extreme or strange, especially to non-Japanese, but it is not unusual for many Japanese corporations. My previous working experience at these Japanese corporations exposed me to this concept strongly. I began my professional career as a salesperson of electronic components, in a Japanese corporation, after earning an university graduation. There were many socialising events for freshmen as mentioned as a common occurrence in the current Japanisation literature. Many of the social events were accompanied with drinks at restaurants, bars and often in the office. What I was taught by managers was to learn how to do business from seniors through socialisation. As freshmen, we were told to frequently go for drinks with seniors as part of our primary duties. One of the experiences I had, which seemed strange to me at the time, was being encouraged to the point of vomiting. The logic behind getting drunk with my seniors was that it was training for future social events with customers. Salespeople were expected to entertain and treat their customers to dinners and drinks towards maintaining good relationships. This business custom is called *seltutai* ('wining and dining customers'). At that moment, I was not convinced about the process of being drunk but tried to make myself as socialble as possible. For me, it seemed to be the only way of surviving at that organisation. A year later, when I was dispatched to a local sales office in Nagoya, located between Tokyo and Osaka, a series of drinking events began to overwhelm me. Definitely, these were too many for me to attend, because in a normal week, there would be several drinking parties, or at least one, after work. I started getting frustrated with these events.

It was not until one event happened that I realised how important these events are in the workplace. There was a symbolic drinking party in Nagoya one night. Around 9 pm, my superiors in another department suddenly popped up at my apartment. I opened the door when the doorbell rang to be met by two superiors standing there. They just told me to get ready to go for drinks. I did not feel like drinking that night and was not submissive enough to follow their order, even feeling anger as to why I had to go out for drinks at that time of the night. So I immediately declined by saying, 'I'm so sorry but I do not want to go because it is too late for me.' They were not convinced and insisted that I come out with them. They tried hard to persuade me by saying that there were already other seniors having drinks in a karaoke bar, I continued to decline and give many reasons for not wanting drink that evening. The talk at the door took almost 20 minutes and they finally gave up on taking me out. The next day, I went to the office and met the two superiors. I talked to them and apologised for the night before, but they just greeted me with stiff politeness. After that, they barely talked to me and I began to feel isolated.

It is another part of the Japanese company as family that people stay together physically, longer than just working hours. This is not limited only to business days. During my days in Japanese corporations, I was invited to a New Year's Eve party at my manager's home. My colleagues and seniors had dinner and drinks together with his family. I needed to understand that working in Japanese corporations is not just a profession or job but rather the coming together of a small community where the people spend not only official but also private time together. On a larger scale, many large manufacturers manifest the notion of company as family even in their factories. The headquarters of Mazda, located in Hiroshima, in the countryside of Japan, is one case. On the opposite side of the road from Mazda's headquarters is the Mazda Hospital, existing mainly for, albeit not limited to, the employees and the families of Mazda staff. Next to the entrance, there is the Mazda Museum. Toward the north, there is Mazda gymnasium surrounded by Mazda dormitories. Likewise, other automotive companies have similar layouts of their plants and offices. Toyota group corporations are no exception. In their factories, there tend to be gymnasiums, dormitories, a baseball ground, tennis courts and even stores and restaurants for their employees. It is a small community where the workers spend their official and private time together. The concept of company as family, as I've eventually realised, still strongly remains at large Japanese manufacturers.

3 An institutional logic approach and constellations of logics

Family, religion, market and corporation logics

3.1 Introduction

This chapter formulates a conceptual framework to analyse practices across the subsidiaries of a Japanese MNC. The structure of this chapter is divided into two sections. First, the recent development of institutional logics is reviewed. Second, logics that are expected to be enacted within a Japanese MNC are reviewed. In the concluding section, the conceptual framework is summarised. The constellations of logics are adopted with the emphasis on the geographical locations in which practices are conducted. This also shows another 'cultural space' where logics can be in play differently from those that are argued by institutionalists (Thornton et al., 2012). Therefore, logics defined through analyses focused on Western society may not work well in other regions.

3.2 Recent development of an institutional logic approach

This section reviews and evaluates recent developments in the study of institutional logic and constellations of logics. It is divided into three subsections. First, an institutional logic approach is introduced. Next, constellations of logics are discussed. Finally, the relationality of the constellations of logics is elaborated upon. In a summarising subsection, a conceptual framework is identified and the constellations of logics are adopted to analyse practices across the foreign subsidiaries of a Japanese MNC.

3.2.1 The institutional logic approach as a macro analysis

Institutional logic was originally coined in the seminal work of Friedland and Alford (1991). They describe Western society as 'the inter-institutional system' composed of social sectors such as 'Capitalism, Family, Bureaucratic State, Democracy, and Christianity'. They define institutional logic as 'a set of material practices and symbolic constructions – which constitute its organizing principles and which is available to organizations and individuals to elaborate' (p. 248). Each sector has 'a central logic': capitalism as 'accumulation and the commodification of human activity'; family as 'community and the motivation of human activity'; the bureaucratic state as 'rationalization and the regulation of human activity by legal and bureaucratic hierarchies'; democracy as 'participation and the extension of popular control over human activity' and Christianity as 'truth, whether mundane or transcendental, and the symbolic construction of reality within which all human activity take place'.

The institutional logic approach is coined as an explicit critique of the institutional isomorphism that fails to take complexity into consideration. In institutional theory, a concept of institutional isomorphism had been dominant. It was proposed by DiMaggio and Powell (1991, p. 147) as 'a result of processes that make organizations similar without necessarily making them more efficient'. They argue that organisations often adopt the same organisational forms and structures, resulting in increasingly similarity. This similarity is caused not by efficient adaptation to competitive forces from external or technical environments, but by ritual adaptation to a social construction in environments. In a sharp contrast to this isomorphism, Friedland and Alford (1991) suggest institutional logics at the societal level that possibly cause conflicts at the organisational and individual levels in a complex manner. These institutional logics can be identified across three units of analysis: society, organisations and individuals.

> When institutions are in conflict, people may mobilize to defend the symbols and practices of one institution from the implications of changes in others. Or they may attempt to export the symbols and practices of one institution in order to transform another.
>
> (Friedland and Alford, 1991, p. 255)

The symbols and practices are not simply societal effects but also are transformed and even manipulated by individual actors at the organisational level.

Although Friedland and Alford (1991) based these institutional logics at the societal level, Thornton and her colleagues have sought to renew the institutional logic approach. Initially, Thornton (2004) extended the taxonomies of the inter-institutional system, 'institutional logics of societal sectors' to markets, corporations, professions, states, families and Christian religions. She adds 'key characteristics', elements of each logic which are the economic system, symbolic analogy, sources of legitimacy, authority and identity, as the basis of norms, attention and strategy. Furthermore, she replaces democracy logic, defined by Friedland and Alford (1991), with corporation logic by claiming that democracy can be a variable to the corporations, which strive to have a democratic management style with organisational hierarchies.

Recently, Thornton et al. (2012) have proposed a comprehensive matrix of the inter-institutional system comprising two axes: a Y-axis of elements of logics and an X-axis of logics of institutional orders. In this matrix, they define seven logics as family, religion, state, market, profession, corporation, and the newly added community. With reference to the recent studies of community (Marquis et al.,

2007; Marquis and Battilana, 2009), they identify the institutional effects of community, refining this inter-institutional system. Although the original work of Friedland and Alford (1991) aimed to tease out a nuanced notion of institutional logics, distinctive from isomorphism, a series of work by Thornton and colleagues tends to revert the notion of institutional logics to once again be closer to the notion of institutional isomorphism: i.e. a deterministic structure and a summary of macro analyses where a social structure determines individual actors' behaviours by isomorphic pressures.

Furthermore, without giving clear reasons, they drop 'Christian' from 'Christian religions' (2004) and assert the 'religion' logic instead, seemingly characterising other religions as having the same elements as Christianity. Nonetheless, this renewal may have gone too far since it makes assumptions about other religions, such as contemporary Islam or Buddhism, that may not be valid. They point out that the 'cultural space' of modern Islam, for example, can be in conflict with market principles while Christian religion would transform savings and investment into the sign of salvation (Weber, 2010). Moreover, this series of refinements assumes that the inter-institutional system of logics gradually becomes universal, even though it was originally specifically defined as a basis of Western society.

These institutional logics at the societal level have been largely applied to institutional change at the organisational level, where one dominant logic is replaced by another among organisations. Thornton and Ocasio (1999), for instance, identified a shift of institutional logics at the organisation level in the publishing industry in the United States from editorial logic to market logic. Attributes of editorial logic were replaced by those of market logic: personal capitalism was replaced by market capitalism; personal reputation by market position; and increased sales by an increase in profits. Similarly, a historical analysis of accounting firms in Canada by Greenwood and Suddaby (2006) illustrates a shift from professional logic to market logic at the organisation level, leading to new organisational forms, 'the multidisciplinary practice' including accounting, legal and management consulting services. Profession logic was confined to a narrow band of audit services but was replaced by market logic composed of the demands of their clients who expand their business globally. Consequently, a broad range of services, such as a legal service, was established for the sake of responding to clients' needs. This emphasises the effects of societal logics from macro analysis whereby the dominant societal logic is replaced by another among organisations.

One dominant views on this level of analysis has been groups of organisations as the 'organisational fields' whereby the institutional logics from the societal level operate at the organisation level (e.g. Rao et al, 2003; Marquis and Lounsbury, 2007). This view is based on DiMaggio (1991) who defines organisational fields as 'those organizations that, in the aggregate, constitute a recognized area of institutional life: key suppliers, resource and product consumers, regulatory agencies, and other organizations that produce similar services or products (p. 148)'. These macro levels of society and the organisational fields are assumed to enable organisational actors' actions. Reay and Hinings (2009), for instance, describe a healthcare industry as 'the Albert health care field' in Canada. Thornton and Ocasio (1999) also apply the notion of the organisational field to the 'higher publishing industry' in the United States, an organisational field whereby organisations are similar in acquiring their legitimacy in their economic activities. This strand in the literature primarily focuses on macro analysis, although these levels of analysis are nested in a complicated manner of 'individuals competing and negotiating, organizations in conflict and co-ordination, and institutions in contradiction and interdependency (Friedland and Alford, 1991, p. 240–1)'. Nonetheless, the concept of organisational fields can be useful to explain the complexity of Japanisation as Westney (1987) used, and how practices are revised, rejected or transformed in different ways.

Recently, Friedland et al. (2014) asserted that varieties of logics can be in play across different institutions because of a metaphysical category in logics, 'an institutional substance' that can transpose across institutional sectors. Therefore, within a legal institution like the corporation, other logics such as religion and 'family' may come into play. They further elaborate the ontology of institutional logics by denying that they are simply mere subjects, objects or practices, and instead affirming that they are built 'through a metaphysical category – an institutional substance'. They assert that '(i)nstitutional substances are not values per se, but rather institutional objects enacted and thereby valorized through practice, that is through the simple fact of their production' (p. 333). Logic is 'a social construct, a substance enacted in practices by which one gains access to it, affording emotions and affects that substantialize it' (p. 337), which places a strong emphasis on an institutional substance embodied by practices.

3.2.2 *Constellations of logics as cooperative and competitive relationships among logics*

Recently, some scholars have begun to question the dominant literature of institutional logics and institutional change as a macro analysis whereby there has been a shift from one logic to another logic. In particular, Goodrick and Reay (2011) propose constellations of institutional logics as 'the combination of institutional logics guiding behavior at any one point of time (p. 399)'. Like 'a configuration or positions of "stars"' in the sky, multiple logics can coexist, guide actors' behaviours and eventually be identified as patterns of cooperative and competitive logics.

By conducting a longitudinal study of the professional work of pharmacists in the United States since 1852, Goodrick and Reay (2011) describe how the constellation of logics guides professional actors and their work in each era. The logics discussed are the market, professional, state and corporation logics. Through five eras, each approximately several decades, they analysed 'a set of logics in a recognisable pattern' and identified three constellations of logics: one with a single dominant logic, where the other three do not guide behaviours; another with two significant logics and the other two with a less significant influence; and a third constellation, with one logic moderating three other less influential logics. The difference between dominance and moderation is visualised as the extent to which each logic is positioned higher or lower than the others. Primary attention is given to the relationships between more than two coexisting logics. Unlike the previous literature that argued for two logics with one 'winning' and other 'losing', this is a useful concept that assumes multiple coexisting logics and 'their collective influence on a social actor'.

Through this strong emphasis on the effects of more than two coexisting multiple logics, they argue for constellations of logics composed of cooperative as well as competitive relationships. The competitive relationship is a 'zero sum' where there is an equal amount of gain and loss of logics in the available 'pie', whereas the cooperative relationship is 'non-zero sum' where there is a gain of multiple logics and possibly an expanded 'available pie'. Although what the pie means was not fully clarified by them, their approach entails a comprehensive concept of dealing with multiple logics.

More recently, Waldorff, Reay and Goodrick (2013) further elaborated on the mechanisms of the constellations of logics, which enable as well as constrain actors' actions. Adopting a comparative case study of healthcare initiatives at micro and macro levels in Denmark and Canada, they conclude that two mechanisms, such as the 'presence of an influential logic' and an 'additive relationship between logics', enable actors' actions and eventually institutional change, while three mechanisms, such as 'strengthening alternative logics', 'segmenting competitive logics', and 'facilitative relationships' constrain actors' actions and, in turn, institutional stability. Unlike their previous study, which focused on the professional work of pharmacists, this work extends its scope to the organisational fields in the healthcare industry as a whole. These mechanisms, however, can be contextually triggered according to actors in their contexts because the actors decide these relationships among logics (Smets and Jarzabkowski, 2013). Thornton et al. (2012) briefly touch upon actors' actions as 'partial autonomy', albeit not elaborating it further. Given enabled and constrained actors' actions through the constellations of logics, ceremonial aspects through boundaries of logic, as well as the cooperative and competitive relationships, are discussed next.

3.2.2.1 Cooperative relationships among multiple logics

The cooperative relationship among logics – in other words, the 'win-win' relationship – has been rarely discussed by institutionalists. Therefore, the strengthening of one logic does not imply a corresponding weakening of another logic. Goodrick and Reay (2011) elaborate on these 'non-zero sum' cooperative relationships in two different ways: as either 'facilitative' or 'additive' relationships. The facilitative relationship means that multiple logics gain collective influence to guide practices. In their study, customer knowledge of medication acquired through the Internet and advertisements (the market logic) supported pharmacists' abstract knowledge (the professional logic) as the pharmacists interact with customers. Thus, one logic can facilitate another logic. In contrast, the additive relationship means that multiple logics guide different expectations that do not necessarily present conflicting demands. Goodrick and Reay (2011) explain that the pharmacists at some point needed to show both professional competence and an ability to meet customer expectations. Both professional and market standards are not conflicting but simply additive in the sense that they are two different standards guided by the professional and market logics. Thus, one logic can be added to another logic.

This concept of the cooperative relationship alongside the competitive one is useful in illuminating culturally complex meanings in respect to practices. It certainly helps to describe and explain the ebbs and flows of coexisting multiple logics through the dynamic relationships among logics. Both the 'facilitative' and 'additive' concepts, however, may not generally be used in practice unless a group of actors has to be narrowly limited. In their case, pharmacists, as the professionals, are the focus of actors, and thus facilitative and additive relationships are easily defined from the view of the pharmacists. Therefore, for surrounding groups of professionals, such as nurses and medical doctors, these relationships may not be the same as those of pharmacists. For instance, the facilitative relationship for a doctor may be additive for a pharmacist. Thus, these two relationships have to be examined with great caution. Furthermore, the distinction between facilitative and additive relationships may be further blurred: Waldorff, Reay and Goodrick (2013) argue for 'facilitative relationships' additionally meaning 'strengthening one logic serves to strengthen another logic', while Goodrick and Reay (2011) originally argued for 'additive relationships' as extending the 'pie'.

A more useful concept can be that of the 'amplified' effects of logics used by Greenwood et al. (2011). They lend support to amplified effects by questioning: 'whether the logics of family and religion, when they occur together, amplify each other's effects because of their common theme of social responsibility and their antipathy to the more individualized implications of the neoliberal market logic (Greenwood et al., 2010, p. 527)'. Their study concerns the case of 'family' firms in Spain, describing the organisational environments surrounding the Spanish manufacturing industry. Using quantitative analysis of the downsizing of the Spanish manufacturing sector between 1994 and 2000, they examine the interrelationships among the market, family and state logics. Then they conclude that the market logic, specifically originating from small- to medium-sized enterprises, is mediated by non-market logics, which occurs directly through the 'family' logic and state logics and indirectly through the religion logic. The fact that 'the relevance of family in Spain is at least partly a function of the Catholic Church (Greenwood et al., 2010, p. 535)' helps to identify the amplified aspects of these logics. Here, in respect to constellations of logics, this study of the amplified logics (Greenwood et al., 2011) is simply considered as 'facilitative relationships' among logics by Waldorff, Reay and Goodrick (2013). Nonetheless, it emphasises the strengthened effect of logics, rather than simply facilitating logics, bringing about a distinction between amplified and facilitative relationships: the former strengthens logics while the latter only facilitates logics without necessarily strengthening them. Although it primarily concerns the heterogeneous effects of multiple logics from macro analysis, the notion of amplified effect can be useful in describing enactments of cooperative relationships among logics through practices.

In Japanese MNCs, the cooperative relationships can be identified with the family, corporation, religion, and market logics because Japanese are considered to view 'company as family' (e.g. Hartvany and Pucik, 1981; Keys and Miller, 1984; Kondo, 1990) (see 2.3). Japanese manufacturing and non-manufacturing practices are underpinned by the notion of family, which is hearth, 'signifying people who belong to the same domestic group (Kondo, p. 121)' and thus, share 'a common destiny' (Kondo, 1990). The notion of family can be recognised especially in Asia, and therefore may be amplified with other logics. Nonetheless, it may not be the case in the Western regions because of their cultural preference for individualism (e.g. Graham, 1994).

3.2.2.2 Competitive relationships among multiple logics

The competitive relationship among two logics, both the 'victory' of one logic and the 'defeat' of another logic, has been frequently discussed by institutionalists. It implies a 'zero sum' where the strengthening of one logic provokes a weakening of the other logic. The concept is associated with early institutionalists such as Thornton and colleagues, who argued for zero sum relationships among logics (e.g. Thornton, 2004). Goodrick and Reay (2011) claim that in competition among logics, there must be an equal amount of both gain and loss in 'the total available "pie"'. Despite no clear definition of what the 'pie' is, the competitive relationship heavily implicates a zero sum relationship among logics, thereby bringing about 'segmented' practices guided by different logics. The concept of 'segmenting' responds to the competitive relationship among logics, arguing that the coexistence of multiple logics results in 'segmenting their impacts on different actors, geographical communities, or types of organisations (p. 379)'. Briefly, each practice is guided by a different logic. Segmenting can be a mechanism that allows competitive logics to coexist by dividing up the total pie, thereby concluding that professional work is segmented by multiple logics. This competitive relationship can include incompatible relationships among logics, such as conflict and tension.

This segmenting echoes 'organisational responses' to 'institutional complexity' (Greenwood et al., 2011). Like the constellations of logics, institutional complexity is built on parts of a critique of the current literature, with its overriding emphasis on a single logic dominating the organisational field. It has different underlying assumptions from the constellations of logics; however, it is limited only to the competitive relationship among logics and it treats primarily 'organisations' as institutional actors. The concept of institutional complexity is based on the competitive relationship between logics in reference to 'the number of logics and the degree of incompatibility between them' (p. 334). In their study, a response can be the 'partitioning/compartmentalising' of an organisational unit into different norms, practices, processes and mindsets. These parts of the 'organisational response' to institutional complexity are generated in the organisational field.

Furthermore, the conceptualisation of complexity is based on the assumption that organisations are institutional actors, placing a high priority on macro analysis. They go on to argue that multiple institutional logics at a societal level can be played out at the organisational and intraorganisational level. This demand is an outgrowth from their assumption that not all organisations receive institutional pressure equally at the organisational field level because organisational arrangements serve to filter complexity. Although institutional complexity has a limited focus on only the competitive relationship and organisational actors, the concept of 'partitioning/compartmentalising' (Greenwood et al., 2011) may help to explain how logics are fragmented within 'organisations'.

Other possible responses to the competitive relationship among logics can be 'actors' active collaboration'. With the case study of health organisations in Canada, Reay and Hinings (2005) describe coexisting logics as part of institutional change, focusing on the empirical investigation into how a field can be reestablished after institutional change. Later, they develop this investigation of the question of how to manage competing logics. Reay and Hinings (2009) clarify that favouring conditions of dealing with competing logics can be 'mechanisms for managing the rivalry of competing'. They identify conditions that make the coexistence of multiple logics possible. That is, multiple coexisting logics can be managed through collaborations of actors because active collaboration by actors can resolve the contradiction and conflicts that can be introduced by the rivalry of competing logics. Their argument is based on actors' voluntary actions and motives to manage institutional logics, rather than on norms and myths in institutionalism, which shape actors' actions.

In Japanese MNCs, the competitive relationships among logics are estimated to be identified in the foreign subsidiaries of Japanese MNCs, especially in Western regions, as the unsuccessful cases of transferring Japanese management practices imply (Elger and Smith, 1994; 2005). In particular, the 'family' logic associated with group orientation and collective responsibility might sharply conflict with independent individuals based on market logic (e.g. Graham, 1994). By contrast, in Asia, the competitive relationship can be minimal.

3.2.2.3 Ceremonial aspects through boundaries of logics

Meyer and Rowan (1977) define ceremonial aspects deriving from formal organisational structures that reflect on institutional rules as myths. They argue that organisations need to incorporate institutional rules gaining legitimacy from society to survive in those environments. The ceremonial organisational structures are due largely to inconsistencies between technological efficiency (market logic) and institutionalised organisational structure (corporation logic). This proposition of Meyer and Rowan (1977) was supported by the work of Westphal and Zajac (1998) that examined the share price of corporations. Adopting a quantitative method, they discovered that the price went up when the corporations adopted a legitimate practice such as 'long-term incentive plans', regardless of whether they implement it or not. This indicates that their adoption was principally a ceremonial corporate practice. Similarly, Oliver (1990) positions these ceremonial organisational structures as distinct from real activities because of the 'strategic responses' to institutional process. Following Oliver, Greenwood et al. (2011) rephrase it as 'organisational responses' to institutional complexity.

In the constellations of logics, the ceremonial aspects emerge because of 'segmenting' logics. Goodrick and Reay (2011) indicate the complexity of coexisting logics by showing that some dimension of the professional work of pharmacists enacts different logics, thus segmenting their impact on practices. The pharmacists' work is manifested through segmenting the professional logic (their professional competence in pharmaceutical knowledge) and the market logic (the commercial ability to meet customers' expectations about medicinal drugs). As Meyer and Rowan (1977) argue, however, while ceremonial aspects are expected to emerge in particular through segmented inconsistencies between efficiency (market logic) and organisational structure (corporation logic), this may not always be the case in respect to constellations of logics that comprise more than these two logics. Not only do other logics, such as family and religion logics, affect ceremonial aspects, but they can also be sources of inconsistencies causing ceremonial aspects. This segmenting assumes the intimate relation between logics and 'different actors, geographical communities, or types of organisations', rather than within intraorganisations.

Furthermore, articulating this segmenting as 'compartmentalisation' Greenwood et al. (2011, p. 342) touch on the existence of organisational communities by stating that '(t)he structural division of this sense, creates intra-organizational communities which, connected to field-level occupational communities, are "quite likely to differ in their awareness of, and receptivity to, institutional pressures"'. The concept of organisational communities assumes the organisational field level structure influences 'organisational actors', in their words, at the organisational level. Greenwood et al. (2011) further imply that these organisational communities are expected to play a key role in 'segmenting' logics, 'compartmentalising' in their words, by representing and importing logics into different 'organisational' units. They further raise the possibility that the receptivity of the organisational communities' members may be affected by 'the thickness of ties' of organisational communities to their organisational fields. The thicker the ties are, the stronger the role they can play.

Focusing on the individual level, rather than on intraorganisational units, Suddaby et al. (2012) sheds light on the actors' profiles of their life histories, which constitute the actors' 'institutional reflexivity'. When analysing the communications consultancy field in France, they reached the conclusion that 'incumbents were able to maintain their position in the social order because of . . . their ongoing understandings' (p. 44). They attribute institutional reflexivity to the actors' life histories, which are social position, expert power and rhetorical skill, by arguing that:

> Variations in one's personal biography, thus, may afford greater institutional reflexivity because of their social position, their educational history, their network relationships, their hierarchical position within organizations and a host of other factors that differentially expose some to higher degrees of reflexivity than others.
>
> (p. 13)

Thus, actors' profiles can be a key to achieving institutional reflexivity to surrounding institutional environments. In institutional logics, this finding strongly echoes the work of Battilana and Dorado (2010), which illuminates actors' profiles of conducting practices enacting a particular logic. Conducting comparative analysis between successful and failed microfinance banks in Bolivia, they conclude that the particular logic manifested by the previous experience of hired employees ultimately prevented them from acquiring other ways of working, and thus becoming a successful bank.

For Japanese MNCs, Japanese expatriates can be organisational communities who are closely associated with 'a field level family logic' to the subsidiaries (Elger and Smith, 2005; Greenwood et al., 2011). The family logic is considered to be bounded to only Japanese communities and thus may allow only Japanese expatriates to be *uchi*, or the 'inner group' of family members. Their ethnocentric structures, whereby Japanese expatriates play a dominant decision-making role (Kopp, 1999), echoes the idea of 'two management structures' between the Japanese and locals (Elger and Smith, 2005). Actors' profiles of organisational communities, however, play an important role in referring back to the organisational fields (Suddaby et al., 2012). A key point can be whether actors have experience in conducting Japanese management practices enacting family logic in their profile. This experience may provoke ceremonial aspects of work organisation since, as Kopp (1999) indicates, Japanese expatriate managers dominate the decision-making process in the subsidiaries while local managers are only slightly involved.

3.2.3 Relationality of constellations of logics in Asia and the West

Constellations of logics are useful in unpacking the nuanced relationships between more than two logics. One emerging issue from a workable definition of these competitive and cooperative relationships, however, is what makes logics incompatible or compatible. The source of both 'incompatibility' and 'compatibility' between logics does not rest on the logics themselves but on the actors conducting particular practices (e.g. Smets and Jarzabkowski, 2013). It is crucial to understand how actors in their contexts reproduce, resist and transform practices through the constellations of logics.

Granted, the constellations of logics unpack multiple logics operating in certain contexts, such as the work of professional pharmacists built on cooperative as well as competitive relationships among multiple logics. Notwithstanding this strong emphasis on varieties of multiple logics, it may lead to reified constellations confined to one historical context only. The constellations are not given by society, rather constellations are assumed to be generated through individual actors' actions and identification. Hallett and Ventresca (2006) argue for 'inhabited institutions' rather than institutions carried by logics. They claim that institutions are not just an 'inert container of meaning' through logics but that they are 'inhabited' by individual actors. The term 'inhabited institutions' helps to explain the notion of constellations of logics from the individual actor's view. This relationality of the constellations of logics can be investigated in depth as individual actor's products and individual actor's enablements and constraints.

The relationality is also ensured by the 'geographical communities' in which particular institutional logics are rooted (Lounsbury, 2007; Marquis and Lounsbury, 2007). By exploring a case study in which a national bank acquires local banks across a number of states, Marquis and Lounsbury (2007) show that particular institutional logics can be embedded in geographically different locations. They examine the tension of competing logics between national and community logics: a 'community' logic of local autonomy focuses on the avoidance of financial consolidation, whereas a 'national' logic of economic efficiency focuses on geographical diversification through expanding and standardising bank branches. In this case, a community tends to protect local autonomy against a demand to standardise for efficiency. Therefore, the geographical locations where constellations of logics are formed do matter.

In the subsidiaries of MNCs, these geographical locations among home and host countries are highly likely to provide different sets of coexisting logics (Kostova et al., 2008). Geppert et al. (2006) assert that transferring practices from the headquarters to their subsidiaries may cause potential conflicts because the subsidiaries of MNCs are locally embedded in their home and host countries. In institutional theory, this echoes a 'relational institutional analysis', as Delbridge and Edwards (2007) suggest. More recently, Delbridge and Edwards (2013) have also argued that these contexts result in 'conditioned' actions of individual actors and agency due to constellations of logics and institutional complexity consisting of conflicting multiple logics in play together. This assumes that actions and agency are 'evolving through time' according to each relational context. This context surrounding different institutional environments should have a different set of constellations of logics. The geographical communities in Japanese MNCs can be all the non-Japanese actors, such as local employees and local customers, who have nothing to do with the Japanese, and are therefore divided by two managements (Elger and Smith, 2005).

Furthermore, in Japanese MNCs, family logic is manifested in company as family (Kondo, 1990), which strongly implicates the relationality of logics themselves because the concept of institutional logic was coined from the analysis of

Western society, not Japanese society. Friedland and Alford (1991) remind us of the limitation of their model by stating that people in non-Western societies 'are less likely to conceptualize individuals independently of the roles they occupy and the contexts in which they are sustained (p. 239)'. In particular, the application of logics to Japanese MNCs needs to pay more attention to surrounding contexts, since they posit that:

> In Japan, a highly industrialized nation, the concept of individualism was a foreign introduction, for which there is still no adequate translation. Its translation still has the pejorative connotation of self-centeredness. For whatever reason, some societies do not conceptualize, let along value, an abstract individual. Clearly, the achievement of individuality was as much a cultural transformation as it was the natural outcome of the division of labor.
>
> (Friedland and Alford, 1991, p. 239)

Thus, institutional logics need to be applied with attention to the geographical locations of Japanese MNCs in both home and host countries. This echoes the 'cultural space' warranted by Thornton et al. (2012), who raise the possibility of a national culture.

This case occurs especially in Western regions where the preference is for individuality rather than the collective identifies of Japanese actors (Kondo, 1990). Comparing Japanese identities with American ones, Kondo (1990, p. 22) identifies the existence of collective identities in Japan when reporting a comment from an informant that 'Japanese don't treat themselves as important, do they? (p. 22)'. She continues to reflect on the significance of the comment by stating that:

> Not only did it perfectly capture my own feelings being bound by social obligation, living my life for others, it also indicated to me a profoundly different way of thinking about the relationship between selves and the social world. Persons seemed to be constituted in and through social relations and obligations to others. Selves and society did not seem to be separated entities; rather the boundaries were blurred.
>
> (p. 22)

If so, then the relationality is profoundly taken into consideration when adopting institutional logics. As a Japanese American, her view stems from comparison and contrast between American interpretations of 'individuality' and Japanese interpretation of selves 'constituted in' society. This echoes company as family where the boundary between the two axes is blurred (Kondo, 1990). Indeed, this illuminates the new 'cultural space' which Thornton et al. (2012) articulate as logics operating in a cultural manner. Thus, institutional logics need to be considered together with their relationality in Asia and the West, and this possibly addresses their limitations.

3.3 The enactment of corporation, market, family and religion logics

This section elaborates on the types of logics enacted within Japanese MNCs through the constellations of logics. Drawing on Friedland and Thornton's arguments, it adds relational components of Japanese MNCs. From an institutional logics perspective, Japanese MNCs are corporations where the legitimacy of corporation logic, or 'market position', is the top priority. Corporation logic concerns the 'market position of the firm' in order to 'increase size and diversification' (Thornton et al. 2012). The corporation logic can impose overarching assumptions onto and within economic organisations such as Japanese MNCs in relation to the market and non-market logics. Important elements of the logics are 'root metaphor', 'source of legitimacy' and 'basis of norms/attention/strategy'. These elements reflect how interpersonal relationships are interpreted in practice within the corporation: root metaphor and legitimacy help to characterise the interpersonal relationship of individuals on organisational practices while norms, attention and strategy support or connect to organisational goals. Table 3.1 summarises selected elements of logics from Thornton and colleagues.

This section is broken into four subsections. First, family logic is reviewed. Second, corporation logic is considered. This is the overarching logic because a Japanese MNC is a corporation, 'a legal institution' in other words. Third, market logic is reviewed. Finally, religion logic is presented. In a summarising subsection, these logics and possible examples are summarised.

3.3.1 Family logic: unconditional loyalty over self-interest

Family logic concerns 'community and the motivation of human activity by unconditional loyalty to its members and their reproductive needs (Friedland and Alford, 1991, p. 248)'. In practice, it assumes 'families attempt to convert

Table 3.1 The definition of institutional logics (Thornton et al., 2012)

Logics	Corporation	Market	Family	Religion
Root metaphor	Corporation as hierarchy	Transaction	Family as firm	Temple as bank
Source of legitimacy	Market position of firm	Share price	Unconditional loyalty	Importance of faith and sacredness
Basis of norms	Employment in firm	Self-interest	Membership in household	Membership in congregation
Basis of attention	Status in hierarchy	Status in market	Status in household	Relation to supernatural
Basis of strategy	Increase size and diversification of firm	Increase efficiency profit	Increase family honour	Increase religious symbolism and natural events

all social relations into reciprocal and unconditional obligations oriented to the reproduction of "family" members. Families are not infrequently threatened when market-based inequalities, universal bureaucratic rules or religious differences become the basis of affiliation, obligation or loyalty' (Friedland and Alford, 1991, p. 249). Following this characterisation, Thornton et al. (2012) add a series of elements that characterise each logic. For example, 'unconditional loyalty' is its legitimacy, 'membership in household' is its norm, and 'increase family honor' its strategy. In contrast to market logic pf prioritising 'self-interest', 'family' logic tends to prioritise family memberships over individual interests through its organisational performance and code of honour.

In research examining family logic within enterprises, family-owned firms tend to be a typical manifestation of family logic and assume the blood relations in terms of the ownership and governance structure. Thornton et al. (2012) insist that family-owned firms can often be tightly integrated such that interpersonal relations are based on 'unity of will, belief in trust and reciprocity'. Greenwood et al. (2011) specifically illustrate how family logic operates at family-owned firms in Spain and how this mediates and restricts the pressure from market logic. They argue that family-owned firms are less likely to impose layoffs than non-family-owned firms, manifesting the family logic against market logic. Similarly, Chung and Luo (2008) also assume that family logic applies at family-owned firms in contrast to those owned by shareholders from foreign countries, and posit that this brings about distinctive forms of acquisition and restructuring. In general, the body of literature tends to assume that blood relations dictate the enactment of family logic in terms of the ownership and structure of these firms.

Nonetheless, family logic is not confined to only ownership and structure but is often influential among interpersonal relationships within the firms. Edwards et al. (2006), for instance, propose a theoretical framework of how low-value-added (LVA) firms are owned and run by family-operated businesses. The 'fraternal firm', in their words, allows workers participation whereby 'workers' preferences are treated seriously and that workers are not treated as mere factors of production (p. 712)'. This family-like relationship is manifested in the cooperative relationship among employees, suppliers and customers who mutually support each other. Supporting this relationship, Miller et al. (2009) argue for this cooperative relationship within family businesses, which eventually leads to a 'cohesive internal community' within the firms, bringing about deeper and more extensive connections with outside stakeholders. Their comparative research between family businesses and non-family businesses in high-tech industries reveals that family firms have more motivation and loyalty, not just from their employees but also from outside stakeholders.

Likewise, family logic operating within Japanese MNCs, as in the family-owned firms, transposes meanings of family norm among employees, suppliers and customers. For these organisations, family logic is manifested not as a simple form of governance, as in family-owned firms, but as a way of management and of structuring interpersonal relationships, because family logic enables actors to share a common destiny (Kondo, 1990; Bhappu, 2000). However, it is not consistent with the parental altruism identified in Western family firms, which refers to 'a utility function that connects the welfare of one individual to that of others' (Karra et al., 2006, p. 863), rather than 'a moral value that leads individuals to act in the interests of others without the expectations of reward or positive reinforcement in return' (ibid.). Instead, family logic concerns family-like relationships in the sense of how managers treat themselves as well as subordinates in the workplace. In this case, it prioritises collective effort, identity and norms rather than individual effort, identity and norms.

In fact, this Japanese version of family logic can be distinctive from that of Western society, mainly because the logic used has come about not only in Japanese society but also in Japanese enterprises. According to Bhappu (2000), the concept of the family is historically embedded in merchants' families in Japanese society. Since the Edo Period in seventeenth-century Japan, the concept of the family has functioned as a social institution because 'the "*ie*" is the material assets of the family, as well as its prestige, class, and ranking in society' (Bhappu, 2000, p. 410). This family logic is assumed to be influential in Japanese MNCs as well as Japanese society. Furthermore, historically elaborating on family logic and interpersonal relationships Bhappu (2000) gives a clear account of the family in Japan where Japanese *ko* and *on* relationships characterise reciprocity and obligation within Japanese corporations:

> The system of pay and promotion rewards seniority within the organizational hierarchy. Achievement is secondary to trust, in keeping with the tradition of the *ie*. Lifetime employment guarantees are extended to employees as *on* in exchange for the employees' subordination, *ko*, to the needs of the organization.
>
> (p. 413)

This articulation of family logic echoes a series of Japanese management practices oriented toward harmony and collectivism (Elger and Smith, 2005). Furthermore, in the Japanese language, the concept of *ko* and *on* relationships is strongly implicated in the terms of *oyabun* and *kobun* (Ishino, 1953) and *ongaeshi*, which characterise interpersonal relationships. This *ko* and *on* relationship, which is based on 'reciprocity and obligation', is shared with the Chinese family norm of *guanxi* (Chung and Hamilton, 2001). These practices are distinctive from those of the Western approach to management (Elger and Smith, 2005). Thus, family logic can be exemplified through harmony and collectivism oriented practices such as seniority, teamwork, long-term employment and sharing information.

In the foreign subsidiaries of Japanese MNCs, family logic may be different between the Asian and the Western regions. It may cause conflict and competitive relationships with other logics in the West, or may not operate at all, while it may take the form of cooperative relationships in Asia. In the Western regions, family refers to 'a utility function' (Karra et al., 2006); thus, it may not coexist with the corporation, market and religion logics. Even if it does, the competitive relationships are expected to be identified. In contrast, family logic in Asia can enable reciprocity and obligation through the cooperative relationships, as in Japan. It may enable the corporation, market and religion logics to coexist.

3.3.2 Corporation logic: organisational hierarchies for market position

Corporate logic originally stems from democracy, which Friedland and Alford (1991) assert as concerning 'participation and the extension of popular control over humans (Friedland and Alford, 1991, p. 248)'. In practice, it assumes that 'parliaments and electoral institutions convert the most diverse issues into decisions that can be made either by majority vote or consensus among participants, and cannot directly recognize claims of authority based on technical expertise or class privilege (p. 249)'. Later on, Thornton and her colleagues (Thornton, 2004; Thornton et al., 2012) extend this democracy to 'corporation' logic, because they view democracy as a dependent variable of institutional orders of corporations, not institutional order itself. Rather, they argue that the corporation as 'a legal institution', an independent societal sector, has a democratic way of management within flat hierarchies. Thus, the corporation logic enables individual actors to acquire a dominant 'market position' as their legitimacy for individuals and organisations to raise their statuses in the hierarchy and increase the size of their firms. For Japanese MNCs, the corporation logic is an overarching assumption whereby 'the person becomes an employee, which equates to being under the control of managers (Thornton et al., 2012, p. 55)'. All of the organisational practices and interpersonal relationships can be based on the corporation logic, yet are not limited by it.

In the analysis of corporations, attention was initially given less to the corporation than to government organisations, schools and other non-profit organisations, thus overlooking 'the dominant organizational form: the publicly traded, for-profit corporation (Suddaby et al., 2010, p. 1238)'. Instead, some literature discusses as part of institutional change a shift in logics between profession and corporation logic. Thornton (2004; 2005), for instance, analyse public accounting in the United States, a professional business service to corporations, and conclude that there is a shift from profession logic to corporation logic that led to more state regulation. The profession logic enabled accounting firms to sell the legitimacy of financial statements for public corporations. The job of accountants is to protect the 'public trust' of their clients. Nonetheless, after World War II, a consolidation of accounting firms was triggered by the action of the Federal Trade Commission that promoted competition and bidding among accounting firms. Then, the corporation logic emerged to enable the accountants to sell additional services such as legal and management consultancy as 'a salesperson', not 'an auditor'.

In Japanese MNCs, the company as family possibly manifests the tight link in the cooperative relationship between the corporation and family logics because the family is hearth, 'signifying people who belong to the same domestic group

(Kondo, 1990, p. 121)'. Generating profits by corporations is enhanced because of reciprocal obligations among their 'family' members. Japanese management practices, such as seniority, manifest the corporation logic in relation to the family logic. Nonetheless, the relationships among the logics need to be scrutinised in Asia and the West.

3.3.3 Market logic: individual actors' self-interests

Market logic concerns the 'accumulation and the commodification of human activity (Friedland and Alford, 1991, p. 248)'. In practice, it assumes that 'commodity producers attempt to convert all actions into the buying and selling of commodities that have a monetary price . . . capitalist firms cannot exchange unpriced human activities that may be rational for an organization or useful to individuals' (Friedland and Alford, 1991, p. 249). Following this articulation, Thornton et al. (2004; 2012) explore this further: for them, 'share price' is its legitimacy; 'self-interest' is the basis of norms; 'status in market' is the basis of attention; 'increase economic efficiency' is basis of strategy. Based on the fundamental operation of corporation logic, market logic enables actors to conduct the exchange of their labour and its outcome, possibly manifesting in the contract of employment and job description that confirms the commercial nature of the job within the corporation. It is based on an exchange of employees' labour for their outcome, namely the salary they might get. Possible market logic operating practices are an efficient organisational structure, roles and responsibilities, and performance appraisal and salary.

The current literature argues for the market logic as part of a shift of logics or competition among logics (e.g. Thornton and Ocasio, 1999; Lounsbury, 2002; Thornton, 2002; Reay and Hinnings, 2005; Greenwood et al., 2010). For example, Thornton and Ocasio (1999) described a shift from professional logic to market logic at the organisational level in the publishing industry in the United States. The professions of editorial work were replaced by market logic, enabling actors to pursue economic efficiency, profit over revenue. Focusing on the organisational level logics, this strand in the literature describes a shift from profession logic to market logic that enabled organisational actors to increase economic efficiency and grow revenue.

In Japanese MNCs, company as family possibly manifests the cooperative relationship between the market and family logics because family members might be constituted in the company (Kondo, 1990). Nonetheless, the market logic in their foreign subsidiaries might be enacted differently according to different geographical locations. In the West, the self-interest of independent individuals in respect to the market logic may generate a competitive relationship with family logic, which prioritises collective responsibility and collective identities. In contrast, in Asia, it may generate a cooperative relationship with family logic based on the group orientation in Asian regions (Hofstede, 2010).

3.3.4 Religion logic: each religious faith and worship

The religion logic as originally defined was based on Christianity. Friedland and Alford (1991) argued that 'contemporary Christian religions attempt to convert all issues into expressions of absolute moral principles accepted voluntarily on faith and grounded in a particular cosmogony (p. 249)'. Later, Thornton et al. (2012) broadened this focus from the Christian religion, referring simply to a 'religion' logic, and seeking to extract the significance of religion in general. They add a root metaphor to the religion logic, 'temple as bank', which is legitimated by 'faith and sacredness in economy and society', although they do not clarify what the metaphor of 'temple as bank' means. This approach implies the universality of institutional logic perspectives, but a universality that originates only from the analysis of Western society. As a critique of Friedland (2012), Thornton et al. (2012) questions the legitimacy of this religion with reference to the importance of value in logics, proposing religion as simply being 'God'. It seems that both authors assume that the religion logic primarily concerns Christianity in Western society. Notwithstanding this implicit assumption, Thornton et al. (2012) eventually turn institutional logic perspectives forged in Western society into a universal framework: a set of organising principles that guide the actions of actors anywhere. In Asian societies, for example, other religions such as Buddhism and Islam are dominant, and these possibly generate different effects from those of Christianity.

Granted, in empirical studies of institutional logic, religion logic is often based on Christianity. For instance, Greenwood et al. (2010) demonstrate that the implicit effects of Catholicism are accompanied by family logic through restricting the processes of family-owned firms in Spain. In their historical analysis of restructuring small- to medium-sized firms in Spain, they illustrate how family and regional state logics, implicitly affected by the regional Catholic Church, tempered market logic. Looking more closely at individual actors, Thornton et al. (2012) illustrate the religion logic in the case of Penney, a retailer in the United States. The founder, Penney, attempted to instill the values of his religious ethics as a management philosophy named the Golden Rule. This rule viewed 'managers and customers as the congregation – managers as associates and customers neighbors (Penney, 1956)' (Thornton et al., 2012, p. 111). Regarding Christianity, there are two main forms: Protestantism and Catholicism. These two forms are the case in the classic literature of Max Weber, who wrote extensively on the 'protestant ethic and the spirit of capitalism' (Weber, 2010). This work does not elaborate on Protestantism per se but establishes an interplay of logics to demonstrate how a religion logic based on Protestantism enables actors to engage in a market logic based on capitalism. The accumulation of wealth and investment are considered to be a sign of salvation in Protestantism. Similarly, Mutch (2009) claims that a complementary relationship exists between market and religion logics. Analysing the historical development of church governance in the Presbyterian Church of Scotland, he argues that the practices of accountability and record keeping enforce theological beliefs among members, establishing a complementary relationship.

Thornton et al. (2012) realise that there is a 'cultural space' that serves to vary and disturb the effects of institutional logics, either inside or outside of Western society. They suspect that the cultural conditioning of the religion logics produced in, for example, Islam are unlike that of Protestantism and may be in conflict with economic capitalism. It could also be argued, for instance, that Buddhism may or may not be in conflict with the concepts central to Christianity. It is imperative that when institutionalists refer to religion logic or logics they identify the strand of logic concerned and clarify precisely the religion to which they are referring. Summarising the wide variety of religions into one logic may lead to a simplistic view of religion.

In the studies of Japanese management, the Christian ethic does not apply. Rather, Confucianism alongside Buddhism and *Shinto* (Japanese ritual observances and sacred sites) are more likely to shape Japanese values (e.g. Kondo, 1990). Bhappu (2000) argues for recognition of the strong influence of Confucianism, which has historically resided in the concept of family in Japan. She states that this Japanese version of Confucianism was combined 'dominance-submission relations' in China with European rights and duties deriving from feudalism. This manifests the concept of *ko* and *on* relationships in the Japanese family in the sense that while *ko* concerns children's duty to their parents, *on* concerns their reciprocal obligation as family members. This relationship has been historically evident and was also included in the Meiji Civic Code, which marked a shift from the Samurai Era to the Meiji Restoration. The educational policy of the code, the Imperial Rescript on Education, gave Confucian teachings top priority as the historical assets of the Japanese Emperors, thereby raising the importance of Confucianist values: respect for elders and parents and harmony within the social group. In modern management practices, this emphasises 'patience', 'the respect of elders', 'upholding the family' (Beechler and Bird, 1999), possibly replacing Christian faith and worship with one's relationship with one's surrounding people. It is doubtful, therefore, to assume that ethics represented by the Christian faith exist in the same way in the relational contexts where Confucianism is dominant.

Similarly, the tenets of Christian faith and worship may not be useful in contexts where Buddhism is dominant because faith in Christianity is based on the existence of God, but this is not the case in Buddhism. Buddhism does not have a concept of God as the world creator, but instead has 'karma' – the cause and effect relationship constituting the world. For instance, in Thailand, where Theravada Buddhism is dominant, Atmiyanandana and Lawler (2003) point out that:

> Buddhists believe that karma (the sum of both good and bad deeds one achieves during life) helps determine one's next life and most Thais seem concerned mainly with achieving a good "next life" rather than the blissful state of nirvana. . . . The centrality of Buddhism means that values

associated with acquiring positive karma (merit), such as kindness towards others, particularly the less fortunate, has a strong influence on managerial behaviour: the ideal Thai leader is seen as more of a benevolent father than an autocrat.

(p. 234)

In this sense, it may be fair to say that attention in Buddhism may be oriented more to surrounding people rather than to God. Furthermore, Buddhism assumes an endless cycle of death and rebirth while Christianity has a one-off cycle of birth and death, representing transition to an eternal life. This cultural space for religion logic needs to be considered.

In the foreign subsidiaries in Japanese MNCs, the religion logic may exist differently in Asia and the West, where there are a wide variety of religions. In Asia, the religion logic may generate cooperative relationships with other logics because of the dominant Buddhism and Confucianism. In contrast, in the West, this religion logic enables actors to see individuals express themselves within the collective rather than the individual (e.g. Hofstede, 2010). Similarly, another study points out the effects of the religion logic that flows from Buddhism and Confucianism (Dollinger, 1988) and their role in building the ethics of Japanese management. Japanese management practices, in fact, concern *keiretsu*, seniority and long-term employment, all based somewhat on collectivism. In the West, this may not be the case. In Western society, Christianity is closely associated with individualism in terms of the relationship to God. Thus, the religion logic is deeply rooted in the geographical community of a host country and competes and cooperates with other factors such as family, corporation, and market logics at Japanese MNCs.

3.4 Conclusion

This chapter has presented a conceptual framework for studying practices across the subsidiaries of a Japanese MNC. As a point of departure, the institutional logic approach (Friedland and Alford, 1991; Thornton (2004); Thornton et al., 2012) was reviewed. Constellations of logics (Goodrick and Reay, 2011) was further identified to characterise how practices in a Japanese MNC can be conducted and interpreted. These practices are composed of cooperative as well as competitive relationships among logics. The cooperative relationship implies a win-win of multiple logics while the competitive relationship implies the victory of one logic in exchange for the defeat of another. This scenario also raises possible ceremonial aspects through the boundaries of logics because of the dominant Japanese organisational communities within Japanese MNCs. In addition, the relationality is considered in the constellations of logics because what makes logics cooperative as well as competitive is actors in their contexts in Asia and the West, in that logics are rooted in their 'geographical communities' (Lounsbury, 2007). Across the foreign subsidiaries of a Japanese MNC, geographical locations possibly affect constellations of logics in given practices. This implies that in the subsidiaries of a Japanese MNC, actors interpret and act in various ways according to their relational contexts in their host countries. Friedland and Alford (1991) raise the possibility that the relationality between actors in a Japanese MNC might be guided by different logics than those in Western society where the institutional logics perspective was developed. This difference echoes the 'cultural space' in logics proposed by Thornton et al. (2012).

Within the constellations of logics, the chapter identified and elaborated on family, corporation, market and religion. In particular, non-market logics such as family and religion were identified as areas of focus. Family logic is rooted in Japanese society where Japanese management practices are born and raised. Family logic in Japanese management does not depend on whether a company is owned by a family. Rather, it operates among the interpersonal relationships between management and employees, as reciprocal *ko on* relationships within a firm, characterising the 'company as family' (Kondo, 1990). Lifetime employment, teamwork and consensus orientation are closely associated with family logic. Religion logic, in respect to Confucianism, is a secondary feature of Japanese management practices. Its priorities include respect for elders, which is echoed through a tendency for promotion by seniority. Market logic remains the overarching logic among Japanese MNCs and is fundamental to viewing their economic activities. These logics are targeted to characterise and interpret practices in a Japanese MNC. They are deeply rooted in geographical communities in the subsidiaries of Japanese MNCs.

In Chapter 4, the research method is discussed and the characteristics of logics are further defined in actor conducting practices.

3.5 Personal reflection: religious understandings in Asia and the West

The religious understanding in this chapter reminds me of religious differences between Asia and the West, to be exact, Christianity and other Eastern religions. In Japan, religion concerns a mixture of Buddhism and Confucianism imported from China as well as *Shinto* which, originated of the ancient age of Japan. Unlike religion in the West, life is not a one-off event from birth to death, going forward to either heaven or hell. Furthermore, there is no concept of God, the creator of the world as mentioned in Christianity and neither is there the concept of the truth, which has been developed within the sciences. For many Japanese, as well as for me, the absolute truth is an unfamiliar term. Rarely have I heard of or discussed the word of truth at school or the workplace in Japan. The truth can be interpreted as multiple truths rather than absolute one. Unlike Christianity, which is based on monotheism, Japanese religion is polytheism where Buddhism and Confucianism are mixed and coexist in a basis of *Shinto* as deism. This belief constitutes a sharp contrast to the belief of Christianity where only one God is allowed.

Personally, I sensed this religious difference in daily life in the United Kingdom as a PhD student. Not until hearing the news about the Jimmy Savile scandal in the United Kingdom around 2011 had I known the importance of this religious difference. A previously known TV and radio personality at the BBC in the United Kingdom, Jimmy Savile was alleged for a number of child abuse cases after his death. First, I felt it was awkward and strange. Indeed, this scandal was even hard to understand. Upon reflection, neither was the number of his abuse nor the length of his crime spanning around six decades in his career. What intrigued me was the fact that these criminal allegations happened after his death. I asked myself why the people talked about the dead and even accused of him when he had already passed away. A friend of mine, an English pastor named Jay, explained the details of the news story and why Jimmy Savile was supposed to be accused even after his death. However, a question still comes up in my mind as to how people can talk about the behaviour of a man who passed away already. He is gone! Why are people making an effort to accuse him? Would it make any difference?

My friend's answer concerning Jimmy Savile being criminalised after his death enabled me to see different interpretations about death between Japan and the United Kingdom. In Japan, many Japanese, as I am, are brought up to never speak ill of the dead. Non-Japanese may know the similar phrase in English that you should never speak ill of the dead. There should be a period of grace, after one dies, in which people can say only good things about the person. However, this does not exactly mean in Japanese saying the dead tell no tales although both superficially look the same. In Japan, the people are expected not to speak ill of the dead because the dead are transformed as *Kami-sama* and *Hotoke-sama* in Japanese. Both words are directly translated as 'God' and or 'Buddha' in English, yet are not equivalent. Neither is a world creator nor an achiever of nirvana. Here, one's *Kami-sama* and *Hotoke-sama* are its ancestors, mainly its grandmother and grandfather. Both are believed to play, for example, the role of guardian angel in Christianity, albeit not exactly equivalent, in the person's life. Few people will therefore, say bad things in public about the dead person regardless of whether he or she was even a criminal because they are now guardian angles.

This belief is rooted in a historical development of religions in Japan, such as Buddhism, Confucianism and *Shinto*. My mom is religious and chants the Buddhist sutra every morning. Whenever I visit my parents' home, according to her belief, I still have to pray at two shrines in the house while clapping my hands a few times: one is for *Kami-sama*, the enshrined deity, and the other for my ancestors, my grandmothers and grandfathers. The distinction between both, however, is sometime blurred. Both words, *Kami-sama* and *Hotoke-sama*, are somewhat guardian angels for prayers. Considering the case of Jimmy Savile in the United Kingdom, I estimate that this type of reactions is unlikely to happen in Japan not only because people think speaking ill of the dead is taboo but also because they perceive him as *Kami-sama* and *Hotoke-sama* in Japanese. As far as I understand, I suspect that no one is alleged after his or her death in Japan. That explains, I noticed later, why I took a half year to understand why the case had been big news.

4 Comparative ethnographic case study

4.1 Introduction

This chapter identifies the research design and justifies the research methods to answer the research questions. It is organised into two sections: research design and methods. First, the research design is identified and elaborated upon. Second, the research method is specified and elaborated. In a concluding section, the need for a comparative ethnographic case study is justified and confirmed in line with the research methods.

4.2 Research design

This section discusses and identifies the research design. It is divided into three subsections. First, the ontology and epistemology of institutional logics are defined with practice theory. Second, the purpose and type of research is discussed. Finally, the cases are selected. The subsidiaries of JapanCo are identified in Asia and the West, allowing an understanding of the subjectively created social world through constellations of logics.

4.2.1 Considering ontology and epistemology: constellations of logics and practice theory

Constellations of logics comprise multiple logics in play as 'a set of material practices and symbolic constructions which constitutes its organizing principles' (Friedland and Alford, 1991, p. 248). Earlier institutional researchers, such as Zucker (1977) and Meyer and Rowan (1977), considered them to be socially constructed. Berger and Luckman (1966) presume that what is to be 'rational' is socially constructed rather than existing independently 'out there'. Later, other institutionalists, such as Zilber (2002; 2006), emphasised a social construction-ist approach by stating the 'social becoming' of individual actors. Following this social constructionist tradition, Thornton et al. (2012, p. 10) assert that '[b]y material aspects of institutions, we refer to structures and practices; by symbolic aspects, we refer to ideation and meaning, recognizing that the symbolic and the material are intertwined and constitutive of one another.' This type of constructionist approach does not help one to understand the cultural meanings of practices in depth; however, because it parallels a positivistic approach that defines institutional logics as a social reality 'out there' through pursuing objective 'social facts', such as quantitative analysis (e.g. Thornton, 2004) and clear detailed definitions (e.g. Thornton et al., 2012).

Interpretive epistemology is considered in order to understand how actors make sense of the social world within Japanese MNCs. This approach focuses on understanding how individual actors make sense of 'the world as it is', which is 'the subjectively created social world' (Burrell and Morgan, 1979, p. 28). From a basis in constructionist ontology, interpretive epistemology focuses on actors' subjective interpretations of practices and their shared intersubjective reality. Here, attention is given to an 'interpretive understanding of social action' rather than social forces' external to it (Bryman and Bell, 2011), thereby allowing an understanding of the cultural meanings of practices.

Furthermore, 'practice theory' (Giddens, 1984) is combined with an institutional logic approach, subsuming all levels of analysis, such as individuals, organisations and society (Friedland and Alford, 1991) into a comprehensive concept of 'practices' as an 'ongoing series of practical activities (Giddens, 1976, p. 81)'. Giddens (1984, p. 2) further asserts that the concept 'is neither the experiences of individual actor, nor any form of societal totality, social practices ordered through time and space'. Here, practices are not conceived as mere additional units of analysis but as a micro-cosmos that can reveal multiple logics in play through constellations of logics. In fact, Thornton et al. (2012), albeit presenting practice theory, we still conceive of practices as mere 'tangible focal points' of logics, thereby assuming that the locus of practices can provide a link between social structures and individual and organisational actions. This view obviously retains a residue of positivism and objectivism in the institutional logic approach, and thus emphasises the significance of social structure over that of human agency.

Indeed, the combination between the institutional logics approach and practice theory is a newly emerging approach, which has been labelled the 'practice turn' (Schatzki et al., 2001) and more recently, the 'practice bandwagon' (Corradi et al., 2010). Lawrence et al. (2011) further elaborated on practices as 'both intentional and unintentional outcomes' in the 'everyday getting by of individuals'. Yet, much institutional logic literature, like the work of Thornton and colleagues, treats organisational fields and society as an objective reality that can be achieved through positivistic methods. Interpretive constructionism with practice theory can illuminate the institutional life of a Japanese MNC regarding how individual actors make sense of practices through constellations of logics.

4.2.2 Purpose and type of research: comparative ethnographic case study

The purpose of this research is to understand cultural meanings of practices through constellations of logics across Asia and the West within a Japanese MNC. A comparative ethnographic case study is adopted to aid in understanding cultural meanings in depth. Each of these terms such as comparative, ethnographic or case is justified.

First, the research is a case study. Abercrombie et al. (2000, p. 41) define a case study as "the detailed examination of a single example of a class of phenomena". Thomas (2004, p. 127) also asserts that 'the case study aims for the intensive examination of one of a smaller number of instances of the units of interest'. This 'detailed' and 'intensive' examination of institutional complexity is central to the research. Furthermore, my research question concerning constellations of logics well suits the purpose of case studies as Yin (2003, p. 9) clarifies that ' "how" and "why" questions are more explanatory and likely to lead to the use of case studies . . . as the preferred research strategies'.

Second, the research is also ethnographic in the sense that it adopts 'at home ethnography' (Alvesson, 2009) to understand how actors make sense of practices in the subsidiaries of a Japanese MNC. Ethnography, in general, is the 'intensive empirical investigation of everyday lived cultural reality' (Foley, 2002, p. 472). It investigates 'people in places' (Zussman, 2004) with a 'thick description' (Geertz, 1973). Here, 'at home ethnography' (Alvesson, 2009) refers to 'a study and a text in which the researcher-author describes a cultural setting to which s/he has a "natural access" and in which s/he is an active participant, more or less on equal terms with other participants (p. 159)'. This is not a traditional ethnography, which originally stemmed from anthropology. Yet, it is being applied to organisation studies and sociology.

Although ethnography appears well-suited to understanding cultural meanings through constellations of logics, it has several drawbacks in terms of the process of conducting research, such as 'being time consuming, often personally tiring, and stressful to carry out (Alvesson, 2009, p. 158)'. The period of study for a PhD is limited, so it does not allow for multiple ethnographic studies across Asia and the West, which would consume even more time. In fact, Alvesson criticises conventional ethnography as 'uneconomical'. 'At home ethnography', which 'draws attention to one's own cultural context, what goes on around oneself rather than putting oneself and one's experiences in the centre (p. 160)', helps to reveal what cultural meanings are embodied in a Japanese MNC. Briefly, it is more economical and practical than a conventional ethnography. Thus, the 'at home ethnography' method is adopted.

Finally, the research is also a comparative case study with emphasis on the actors' subjective interpretations. The thick description of a single case may be confined to the specific case and contexts, which may limit the validity of the research. Thus, it is critically important to compare and contrast cultural meanings of practices across Asia and the West. In a sense, a comparative case study is essential to make constellations of logics 'open to interpretation' (Voronov et al., 2013) across different geographical locations. This tactic is consistent with the interpretive approach, which concerns how actors make sense of practices within a Japanese MNC; and how practices are being interpreted rests on different actors in Asia and the West. The study helps to reveal multiple complex cultural meanings by comparing and contrasting meanings across Asia and the West.

Thus, a comparative ethnographic case study is adopted for the research that allows cultural meanings to be compared and contrasted through constellations of logics.

4.2.3 Selecting cases: a Japanese MNC and its subsidiaries

My case selection is based on the large size of multinational Japanese manufacturers whose headquarters are located in Japan and whose overseas subsidiaries operate across multiple countries. The units of the cases are sales offices located across overseas regions, preferably North America, Asia and the European Union. Candidate industries are automotive, equipment and industrial manufacturers.

Given these criteria, the pseudonym 'JapanCo' is selected. JapanCo is one of the clients that my father, as a management consultant and coach, has taught for more than two decades. As his son, as well as a management consultant, I often assisted him and took part in his seminars in corporate training programmes at JapanCo. In a sense, I am not a 'professional stranger' (Agar, 1986) since I have known some managers in this company for more than seven years. I am familiar with their management issues through interactions with my father and them. Some of them have known me more than a decade since they often came to my home when I was young. With my father, I sometimes had dinners and lunches with them and advised them on management issues. As an 'at home ethnographer', I had 'natural access' to JapanCo at the beginning of this research.

My identity in relation to others is confirmed according to the participants' interpretations. A Japanese managing director (MD) in JapanCo in Thailand (JTHAI) used me as a management consultant by requiring practical advice from me. Another Japanese MD in JapanCo Taiwan (JTAIW), although well acquainted with me for more than seven years, treated me as an academic researcher. During the first interview on site, he questioned whether JapanCo's headquarters (JHQ) would formally accept my research. Another Japanese MD in JapanCo EU (JEU) asked me to make a presentation in front of top management in JHQ to explain what the subsidiary should look like. This tendency to perceive me more as a management consultant than a researcher needs to be paid attention to throughout the process of data collection and analysis.

JapanCo is a large industrial manufacturer in Japan with revenue of approximately 200 billion Japanese yen, which is equal to about 1.1 billion pounds sterling (1 pound equals 180 yen). The number of employees is about 9,700 across JapanCo groups, including all of the affiliates and overseas sales offices. It owns 12 major overseas sales offices across Asia, Europe and North America and overseas revenue is around 10 per cent of total JapanCo group revenue. Of these subsidiaries, four are selected for this study: Thailand, Taiwan, Belgium and the United States. The selection criteria was to identify subsidiaries in different regions that were initiated with Greenfield investment, rather than through merger and acquisition. There are only two subsidiaries meeting these criteria in Western countries, namely Belgium and the United States, so both of these countries are automatically selected. In Asia, there are varieties of Japanese ways of doing business in each subsidiary according to a pilot study in JHQ. In order to capture varieties, Thailand and Taiwan were selected. JTHAI (JapanCo Thailand) is managed in a Japanese way while JTAIW (JapanCo Taiwan) is managed in a more Chinese way. Thus, the subsidiaries of JapanCo group in Asia, Europe and North America are JTHAI (JapanCo Thailand); JTAIW (JapanCo Taiwan); JEU (JapanCo Europe); JapanCo America (JUSA).

4.3 Research method

In line with this comparative ethnographic case study approach, this section identifies specific research methods. This section is divided into four subsections. First, the stages of the research are presented. Next, the means of data collection and analysis are discussed. Finally, validity is evaluated. In a concluding section, the research methods confirm that the comparative ethnographic case study is adequately implemented.

4.3.1 Six stages of research

This research is divided into six stages, although these stages are not mutually exclusive because the data collection and analysis were conducted iteratively. Overall, the stages are as follows:

First stage: Pilot study at the headquarters (data collection and analysis)
Second stage: Data analysis and literature review
Third stage: Data collection and analysis in two cases (JTHAI and JTAIW)
Fourth stage: Data analysis and literature review
Fifth stage: Data collection and analysis in two more cases (JEU and JUSA)
Sixth stage: Data analysis and writing up

The first stage was a pilot study at the headquarters of JapanCo that was conducted at the beginning of 2012. Corporate strategy and organisational culture were discussed with the main contacts, the subsidiaries were identified and the site visits arranged. Necessary materials, such as a corporate history book, PR magazines and IR materials were collected. Six interviews were conducted to confirm the existence of Japanese management practices and how they were employed.

The second stage of data analysis and literature review was conducted in the middle of 2012. Employing the information acquired, it was possible to identify that institutional theory could be useful to analyse the complex cultural meanings of practices within JapanCo.

The third stage was data collection and analysis in Asia (JTHAI and JTAIW) from the middle of 2012. Semi-structured and open-ended interviews and participant observations were conducted. Forty-one interviews were conducted across various positions from top to bottom and two official meetings and two days of seminars were observed as a participant. In addition, lunches and dinners were taken together with organisational members. Details of the numbers of inter-views, and the titles of the participants, are provided in the next section.

The fourth stage was data analysis and literature review from the middle of 2012 to the middle of 2013. Content analysis was employed. The data was coded into three broad frames: the subsidiary's history, strategy and structure; views of Japanese expatriates; and views of local employees. The sites were compared and contrasted to generate data as well as various cultural meanings of practices. Then, an institutional logic approach was employed in the data analysis through direct quotes of the meanings of the family, religion, market and corporation logics. This frame was later revised in practice because there were no coherent interpretations from Japanese and local employees.

The fifth stage was data collection in the other two cases (JEU and JUS), from the middle of 2013. Semi-structured and open-ended interviews and participant observations were again conducted. Thirty interviews were conducted across various positions from top to bottom and one official meeting was observed as a participant. In addition, lunches and dinners were taken with members of the organisations.

The sixth stage was data analysis and writing up. The code framework was revised and fixed as three broad categories of practices: customer development; work and employment; and work organisation. The four cases were compared and contrasted to illuminate the different cultural meanings embodied in prac-tices. Additional observations were conducted in management meetings.

4.3.2 Data collection

4.3.2.1 Semi-structured and open-ended interviews

In order to understand cultural meanings through constellations of logics, semi-structured and open-ended interviews were adopted as the main data collection method. As an interviewer, it was necessary to be reflexive in asking questions freely about the meanings of multiple logics. This approach also alters the role of interviewer from being a simple data collector to an active and reflective agent (Mason, 2002). The researcher is active in the sense of examining and actively interacting with the meaning of the topic in the interviews, and reflective in the sense of reflecting on the researchers' position and those of the participants. Semi-structured and open-ended interviews made it possible to interact with interview-ees by asking various questions according to the comments of the respondents, while also reflecting on my role, such as being a consultant as well as an academic researcher and a participant. This structure allows one to understand cultural meanings as part of the subjectively created social world.

Furthermore, semi-structured and open-ended interviews necessarily promote such self-reflexivity among research topics and help in the elaboration of constel-lations of logics as 'the socially constructed, historical patterns (Thornton and Ocasio, 1999, p. 804)'. Baker, 2004 (p. 131) assert that 'the process of inter-viewing is better described not as data "collection", but rather as data "making" or data "generation"'. This is also because 'interviewing is understood as an interactional event in which members draw on their cultural knowledge . . . and interview responses are treated as accounts more than reports' (Baker, 2004, p. 131). Thus, in the interviews, Japanese management practices and their meanings are directly asked. The sample interview questions were as follows:

- Are there any Japaneseness or Japanese management practices here? If so, what are they, and how are they being employed?
- Are these practices being implemented and interpreted as in Japan? If so, how?
- Are there norms of family behind these practices? If so, what are they and how are they being interpreted?

These questions further help an interviewer to be flexible in asking various questions according to comments from the respondent. As Miller and Glassner (1997, p. 104) point out, 'a strength of qualitative interviewing is precisely its capacity to access self-reflexivity among interview subjects, leading to the greater likelihood of the telling of collective stories.'

Self-reflexivity is employed to prevent potentially distorting interview data. Thomas (2004, p. 151) specifies that 'what matters is not that the same words are used, or that questions are presented in the same order, but that the questioner and questioned share the same frame of reference and understand the meanings of their communication in the same ways'. An inconsistent frame of reference for both respondents and interviewers may potentially distort interview data. In this case, my experience as a management consultant at JapanCo was helpful to understand cultural meanings in the specific context of JapanCo. Otherwise, the issue may be not only the frame of reference but also the order of questions and recent experiences. According to Bryman (2008), interviewers have a series of questions in their frame of reference, but they can vary the sequence of questions and ask additional questions depending on the significance of replies. In a sense, this self-reflexivity is especially important for interviews conducted across different geographical contexts where the first language of informants may be neither Japanese nor English.

The self-reflexivity is further employed in terms of the position of the researcher in relation to respondents. My identity from the respondents' perspectives could be as either a management consultant, who has a link to management at headquarters, or an academic researcher who seeks to collect data for his research. On the one hand, as a management consultant, I was asked to advise how to manage local employees by the managing director in JTHAI. Likewise, I was also encouraged, as well as politically used by the president in JEU, to make a presentation regarding my findings in front of top management in JHQ, although I had not yet made this presentation or received a formal request to present it as of the day of the submission of this research. In interviews with some participants, I found that my position as a consultant made the participants defensive in respect to my questions. On the other hand, as an academic researcher, I was treated simply as a PhD student pursuing data for its academic interest, and thus was not welcome in some interviews. In the beginning of an interview, a Japanese president was deeply sceptical about my site visit and asked me whether my research was formally accepted by JHQ. Therefore, the researcher's position and those of its respondents were constantly reflected.

Targeted interviewees were local employees and Japanese expatriates, with positions ranging from top executives to non-managerial employees. Since job titles varied for essentially the same functions, the Table 4.1 provides a comparison of job titles and functions.

The main contacts in each subsidiary were all Japanese expatriates. The order of interviews was first the main contacts, usually Japanese top management, and then local employees. Interviews with Japanese expatriates included facts about subsidiaries as well as their interpretations and meanings. Interviews with local employees focused on specific practices according to the position of the interviewees.

In total, 83 interviews were conducted and transcribed in Japanese with Japanese expatriates and in English with local employees. The length of the interviews was typically one hour, or several hours at maximum.

4.3.2.2 Participant observation

Participant observation was adopted as another data collection method. These terms are strongly associated with each other and thus are hard to distinguish from ethnography (Bryman and Bell, 2011). In fact, participant observation goes beyond the simple act of observation. In the context of at home ethnography, participant observation is rather rephrased as 'observing participant' in the sense that the 'participant comes first and is only occasionally complemented with observation in a research-focused sense (Alvesson, 2009, p. 159)'. This is somewhat true because JapanCo is a corporation with which I have been familiar through my father's business, so participant observation was adopted. Furthermore, participant observation is helpful to avoid the possibility of distorting interview data by misunderstanding the surrounding contexts of the interviews. Hence, participant observation is discussed here as a means of data collection.

Participant observation occurs in both formal and informal settings: corporate seminars, regular meetings, and lunches and dinners. With my father's help, I luckily had the chance to attend and present at his corporate seminars in JTHAI,

Table 4.1 Job titles and their functions

Functions	Job titles
Top management	Managing director (MD), president, director, vice-president (VP)
Middle management	Manager, senior manager, assistant manager
Non-managerial position	Sales, secretary, accountant, etc.

which took place over two days in Bangkok. Participants were sales directors and managers. Furthermore, during my stay at each subsidiary, I had lunches and dinners with participants every day. In a casual manner, I was requested to advise them about some managerial issues at each subsidiary. This complements the weaknesses discussed in interviews, reminding me of the surrounding contexts of the interviewees. It also helped to employ self-reflexivity between the topics and the researcher's positions. I observed 31 events.

4.3.2.3 Documents

As a supplementary method of data collection, public and some internal documents were used. These documents mainly supported an understanding of the surrounding contexts of constellations of logics in each subsidiary, rather than the constellations of logics themselves. The main documents used were public documents, such as investor relationship reports and presentations. Another document was a book called *100 Years of History of JapanCo*, which describes the history of the company from its foundation up to 2012 in 549 pages. Another document was on country presentations made for reporting to management from the subsidiaries. Others were internal documents regarding corporate strategy and marketing in each subsidiary, the internal 'JapanCo Group PR Magazine', and a published book by a former CEO of JapanCo, called *Old JapanCo Strategic Management*.

4.3.3 Data analysis and presentation

As an ethnographer, from the beginning of data collection, I started to analyse data by observing, interviewing, advising and recording events. In other words, all events are apparently interpretive opportunities to understand cultural meanings through constellations of logics. My presupposed knowledge about JapanCo and Japanese management practices, which I acquired from interaction with organisational members and my father, as well as through my professional career, greatly influenced what data was selected and interpreted. Given my focus on the cultural meanings of practices, this focus might influence what I saw and failed to see, meaning that some events might be inappropriately selected over others. An event without apparent conflict or cooperation between cultural meanings might have unintentionally less attention paid to it. This choice contrasts the way of grounded theory, which assumes that data 'stands alone' before the data analysis.

A large quantity of textual data from interviews and formal transcribed meetings was coded by broad categories of practices. CAQDAS (computer-aided qualitative data analysis software) was initially considered but later dismissed as a data analysis tool because the interviews were conducted in two languages: Japanese and English. In addition, the use of a software tool might alienate the researcher from the lived reality, possibly weakening the merits of comparative ethnographic case study (e.g. Kelle, 2004). All of the data was therefore manually and iteratively analysed and then connected and disconnected to constellations of logics where multiple institutional logics manifest as 'motives and vocabularies' of institutional logics and their cultural meanings.

From the beginning of this research, the coding framework evolved continuously. Initially, it was coded by broad categories for each subsidiary: its history, strategy and structure; its sales activities; the actions of Japanese expatriates; and the reactions of local employees. The subjectively created world might be expected to be coherent at some degree within each group of Japanese expatriates and of local employees (see Table 4.2).

Later, this framework became inadequate in relation to the purpose of the research. The actions and views of Japanese and locals were found to be complex and not clear-cut between the Japanese and the locals because there were varieties even among them. Furthermore, two external organisations that greatly affect the existence of Japanese management practices were identified: customers locally and JHQ (the headquarters). Thus, the coding framework was finally fixed by broad practices, such as customer development, work and employment, and work organisation (see Table 4.3).

One problem I encountered in the interviews is the interpretation of the terms used because the interviewees' frame of reference differed from mine. Normally, I started by asking interviewees what Japaneseness exists and why they are Japanese. Then, I elaborate on practices manifesting family logic in their frame of reference. In the actual interviews, however, I was sometimes asked by the interviewees about my interpretation of Japaneseness. In that case, I had to share my understanding of Japanese management practices, which are highly

Table 4.2 Initial coding framework (in Thailand and Taiwan)

Themes	*Codes*
History, strategy and structure	· Relation to Japanese customers · Sales and marketing strategy · Organisational structure
Sales activities	· Pressure from JHQ · Two management structures · Roles of Japanese expatriates · Organisational identities · Artefacts and workplace layout
Views of Japanese expatriates	· Their interests and identities · Their handling of sales pressures from JHQ · Teamwork as family work · Norms and social manner · Their frustrations and irritations
Views of local employees	· Their interests and identities · Japanised locals · Acceptance or rejection of teamwork · Team as family or something else · Compromise and resistance · Religious aspects

Table 4.3 Final coding framework

Themes	Codes
Customer development	· Study group
	· On-the-job training
	· Sales follow-up
Work and employment	· Job delegation
	· Performance appraisal
	· Socialisation
Work organisation	· Communicating expatriate evaluation with JHQ
	· Communicating business results with JHQ
	· Communicating locals' complaints with JHQ

likely to manifest family logic through collectivism, teamwork, organisational harmony, and intensive socialisation. Bell and Willmott (2014) mention that this issue can be related to 'action frame of reference' as Silverman (1970) reminds us that 'people act in terms of their own and not the observer's definition of the situation' (p. 37). Thus, continuously employing self-reflexivity, I tried to build a consistent frame of reference between interviewees and myself during the interviews.

At the last stage of writing up the research, through data analysis, the detailed definitions of the logics embodied by the practices were finally identified, as shown in Table 4.4.

Data is presented based on interactions with my supervisors, colleagues and conference attendances. Granted, I collected data and brought my own findings but translated them into their presentation in my PhD thesis in the light, primarily, of feedback from my supervisors. This eventually conditioned how my findings are presented. Initially, my research was planned as Japanese management studies adopting institutional logics. As my research went through constant feedback from my supervisors, the cultural meanings of the Japanese management practices turned out to be the main focus. In particular, the work of Kondo (1990) was studied at a Cardiff Organisation Research Group (CORGies) meeting on the 29 January 2014, and this event greatly influenced my studies in terms of understanding how actors make sense of practices, rather than simply explaining what makes the practices.

4.3.4 Evaluating validity

Based on positivism, quantitative research is traditionally evaluated by the criteria of validity, reliability and generalisability (Silverman, 2006). However, these criteria cannot be used for an ethnographic account, which provides a thick description of how actors make sense of practices. As an alternative, the concept of 'trustworthiness' is adopted. According to Lincoln and Guba (1985), this concept includes four components: credibility, transferability, dependability and confirmability. First, credibility concerns a 'fit' between the researcher's description and the participants' views. Adopting the frame of reference of the participants, a good fit is pursued to match what the researcher sees with what the participants think and believe. The credibility is enhanced, however, by spending time with the participants and by loosely obtaining various pictures through participation, observation and interviews, both at formal and informal occasions. In this regard, I have known some of the informants for more than seven years through my father.

Second, transferability addresses how the research findings can be transferred to another case, rather than universally generalised. The research aims not to provide a correct interpretation confined only to this case but an interpretation that is 'good enough' to be utilised on another case. This is akin to what Geertz (1973) calls a 'thick description': an account rich with detailed cultural meaning that 'provides others with what they refer to as a database for making judgements about the possible transferability of findings to other milieu' (Bryman and Bell, 2011, p. 398). Furthermore, conducting four ethnographic cases, rather a single one, is crucial because it allows the essential findings to be extracted and compared and contrasted between the cases. This rich set of findings and accounts gives the potential for transferability to another case.

Third, dependability refers to how well the research is documented and 'traceable', rather than replicable. In addition to almost all the interviews and formal meetings, even casual conversations at some dinners and lunches were recorded and transcribed. A short memo was written in each case, developing my analysis. Collected data were constantly coded.

Finally, confirmability indicates the tight link between data and analyses. With constant analysis through data collection, I attempted to be constantly connected the data and codes so that the themes could emerge and refer back to particular practices from the data again. This practice helps researchers to conduct their research in 'good faith'.

This 'trustworthiness' echoes the transactional validity in qualitative research, which is defined by Cho and Trent (2006, p. 321) 'as an interactive process between the researcher, the researched, and the collected data that is aimed at achieving a relatively higher level of accuracy and consensus by means of revisiting facts, feelings, experiences, and values or beliefs collected and interpreted'. In this research, the transactional validity helps to evaluate whether the key findings can be significant and useful for the audience of the research, not only for academic researchers, such as institutionalists and Japanese management scholars, but also for managers who work at or deal with Japanese MNCs. It also examines whether the participants' experiences and interpretations can be meaningful representations within a Japanese MNC.

Table 4.4 The detailed definitions of logics embodied by practices within JapanCo

Elements	Family logic (Japanese)	Religion logic (Theravada Buddhism)	Corporation logic	Market logic
Root metaphor	Company as family	Religious group for making religious merits	Company as a group pursing mutual economic goals	Company as a group of economically efficient independent professionals
Source of legitimacy	Reciprocal and obligation-based relationships (*ko-on*)	Predetermined relationship by karma	Hierarchical relationship formed by titles	Independent relationship formed by self-interest
Basis of norms	Maintaining family memberships by active participation	Religious memberships for religious merit	Asserting authority by titles	Pursuing individual self-interest
Basis of attention	(*Wa*) organisational harmony	Importance of religious merits and organisational harmony	Assigned duty according to titles	Individual and independent performance
Basis of strategy	Sharing others' work, information, reward, time and space in an equal manner	Dividing work, information, reward for making religious merits	Dividing work and protecting own information according to titles	Strictly dividing work to each, and protecting own information for themselves

4.4 Conclusion

This chapter identified the research design and justified the research methods to answer the research questions. The purpose of the research is to understand the cultural meanings of practices through constellations of logics. Comparative ethnographic case study was selected as the main type of research. This is comparative across not only Asia but also the West, where constellations of logics were originally identified and theorised. It also is ethnographic since at home ethnography was adopted. It is important to have 'natural access' to the research target, a Japanese MNC, rather than being 'a professional stranger'. Through my natural settings, JapanCo was selected as a case. The interpretation of data went hand-in-hand with the data collection up to the end of writing the book. Through this iterative process of interpretation, self-reflexivity is promoted and utilised, and the researcher examined and interacted with the meanings of the topic not as 'a neutral data collector' but as an 'active and reflective' agent (Mason, 2002).

Furthermore, in line with the comparative ethnographic case study approach, reliability, validity and generalisability are rejected because they are less relevant to ethnographic study. Instead, 'trustworthiness' (Lincoln and Guba, 1985) is adopted. Four components of trustworthiness are considered: credibility, transferability, dependability and confirmability bearing in mind the primary concern of whether the participants' experiences and interpretations can be meaningful representations within a Japanese MNC.

In Chapter 5, the selected case of JapanCo is introduced. This Japanese MNC is actively internationalising its businesses. Its history, strategy and structure, and its subsidiaries in Asia and the West are presented.

5 Varieties of subsidiaries in Asia and the West

JapanCo

5.1 Introduction

This chapter provides relevant background for interpreting the remaining empirical chapters. Moreover, particular empirical facts have been identified and further selected according to their relevance to the idea of family, religion, market and corporation logics. This chapter is divided into two sections. First, a corporate overview is provided, including the historical development of the company, its strategy and structure, and the ways of managing its subsidiaries. In the second section, the influence of the corporate historical development on each subsidiary – namely JTHAI, JUSA, and JEU, and JTAIW – is discussed. The concluding section summarises the entire chapter. With the alliance partner, AmericaCo, JapanCo is characterised as a unique and atypical Japanese corporation, possibly causing complex cultural meanings in practices through varied constellations of logics.

5.2 JapanCo group: corporate overview

5.2.1 History with AmericaCo

At the time of the research (2012), JapanCo had been an industrial manufacturing business in Japan for 107 years. It is an industrial products manufacturer, whose headquarters is also based in Japan. The company's revenue in 2012 reached approximately 200 billion Japanese yen, which had been stable for the preceding five years, despite that its major market in Japan is gradually shrinking. JapanCo's business domain is industrial products, primarily for buildings and industrial plants, in the company's own words, the 'automation business'. Its slogan is 'human-centered automation' and the company aims to bring the benefits of automated processes in buildings and plants closer to people. In its corporate philosophy, it has four core values: safety, comfort, fulfilment and contributing to global environmental preservation. It pursues these values through 'human-centered automation'.

At first, OldJapanCo was founded in 1907 as a family business and later became a corporation under the son of the founder. According to a book entitled

OldJapanCo, which was the original name of the current JapanCo, the company was established by its founder, described here under the pseudonym 'Takahiro Tanaka', as a family business. It started as a trading business, importing industrial products from the United States for military use. However, in 1934, considering the increasing domestic demand for military products in World War II, the founder decided to change the company from a trading business to a manufacturing one. The company then assembled imported industrial products and sold them to the Japanese government. Because of these sales, in 1945, Takahiro Tanaka was succeeded by his son, 'Toshihiro', to avoid the accusation of being a war criminal.

A significant change came about in 1953 when 'Toshihiko Tanaka' built a strategic alliance with an equity alliance partner, AmericaCo. He had studied in New England in the United States and understood the Anglo-Saxon culture, making it easier for both companies to establish an alliance and, as a result, AmericaCo bought 50 per cent of JapanCo's shares. In this way, the roles of both players were explicitly defined: JapanCo was responsible for developing the Japanese market with the products of both companies, while AmericaCo was responsible for the overseas markets selling the products of JapanCo. The alliance was on an equal footing for both players and there were normally only four or five expatriates from AmericaCo, one of whom was appointed as vice-president of JapanCo. This relationship with AmericaCo lasted from 1953 until 1990, when it was dissolved.

Despite the equal partnership, JapanCo had been extremely reliant on AmericaCo in terms of its international product design and development, as well as its overseas sales. AmericaCo provided the expertise to develop overseas markets and industrial product developments, this manifesting the market logic. One example was when it transferred a product launch method, known as a life cycle control (LCC), which managed the product launch process in four phases: idea initiation, planning, design and sales. At the end of a particular phase, each result and performance was evaluated using a profitability index value (PI value) to examine whether an investment was acceptable from the viewpoint of the shareholders. A PI value indicates whether a given project can generate profits within three years. This value therefore enacts the market logic, where the return and investment are prioritised for the shareholders.

This international business development with AmericaCo makes JapanCo a unique and atypical Japanese corporation different from other Japanese MNCs, which in general undertake international expansion on their own. A book published in 1990 written by the former president of the JapanCo group and entitled *OldJapanCo Strategic Management* represents how unique it was at that time. The book indicates how the management methods of AmericaCo were adopted in JapanCo, and how management issues were tackled and defined. Profiles of JapanCo and AmericaCo, and their histories, are provided in Tables 5.1 and 5.2.

Table 5.1 Profiles of JapanCo and AmericaCo

Items	JapanCo group	AmericaCo group
Revenue (2012)	2 billion JPY	36 billion USD
Ratio of overseas revenue	< = 10%	55%
# of employees	9,700	132,000
# of overseas offices	12	50 (estimated)
Ownership	Japanese institutional investors	Owned 50% of JapanCo, but sold it
Length of operation	107 years	120 years
Type of business	Automation(A), Building(B), and other in-house companies	-
Ratio of local customers	100%	-

Table 5.2 The history of JapanCo

Year	Events of JapanCo
1907	Incorporated OldJapanCo in Tokyo
1934	Started to assemble and manufacture industrial products
1953	Formed a technical alliance with AmericaCo to receive technical support
1954	Formed an equity alliance with AmericaCo (50% share owned by AmericaCo) (board members, joint product design)
1957	Renamed OldJapanAmericaCo and developed overseas business with AmericaCo
1991	Reduced stake of AmericaCo to 25% (AmericaCo restructuring)
1991-	Built overseas subsidiaries in Thailand, Taiwan, US, EU and elsewhere
1999	Assumed original name of OldJapanCo
2003	Bought back all shares from AmericaCo
2004	Merged affiliates, adopted an in-house company (consolidating all subsidiaries in Japan into JapanCo)
2006	Renewed its philosophy and symbol of 'automation and building'
2012	Renamed JapanCo

From 1991 to 2012, JapanCo began to develop an international business of its own following the dissolution of the alliance with AmericaCo. In this period, the alliance was becoming useless; conflicts had arisen between both companies because AmericaCo wanted to access the growing Asian market, which was originally the territory of JapanCo. In addition, AmericaCo was facing difficulties and restructuring its businesses because of losses to its main business. In 1992, an internal document in JapanCo indicated that 'it [was] high time for JapanCo to stand on its own feet in international business independently from AmericaCo'. In 2003, JapanCo bought back all the equity from AmericaCo and dissolved the alliances. Since the 1990s, JapanCo has established a series of overseas sales offices in Asia.

From the point of view of JapanCo, AmericaCo was seen as the father in a family, having cared for and trained JapanCo. Some directors of JapanCo characterised AmericaCo as 'the teacher', 'the big brother', and 'the master' who educated JapanCo as 'an inexperienced child' about how to do international business. An experienced director commenting on an internal newsletter of JapanCo stated in the anniversary book, *JapanCo's 100 Year History*, that after ending the alliance 'we then . . . really got to know how much we had been dependent on the capabilities and resources of AmericaCo to develop overseas markets . . . we now [became] unskilled and [had] scarce resources to develop these overseas markets'.

In 2004, JapanCo consolidated all the domestic affiliates of its building system and factory automation businesses into one single company and adopted a divisional company organisation system, namely, the Advanced Automation Company (AA), the Building Automation Company (AB), and one other.

5.2.2 International business development

5.2.2.1 Corporate strategy

JapanCo's mid-term strategy is to internationalise its business. It also wants to expand its overseas revenue to comprise 30 per cent of total revenue by 2016 from a current position of 11 per cent of the total revenue in 2012. Thus, it is at a relatively early stage of internationalisation.

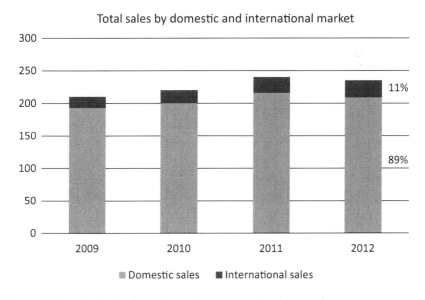

Figure 5.1 Total sales by domestic and international market (billion JPY)

JapanCo adopted a complicated divisional system, controlling each company division as an independent business unit accountable for its own profits and losses as well as its investments. There are two company divisions: Advanced Automation (AA) and Building Automation (BA) (see Figure 5.2). The revenue of both companies is close to 100 billion Japanese yen; AA's business used to be a major source of business that followed that of AmericaCo; BA's business, for its part, was essentially small but, after the acquisition of a domestic building system company, has recently grown, and now has 46 per cent of the total sales (while AA has 37 per cent). AA's business focuses on the factory automation market; its products are sensors, switches, air-conditioning systems and valves. This growth is largely attributed to the influence of AmericaCo's business. In contrast, BA's area of business focuses on the construction industry with products such as air conditioning systems and security products for buildings. This growth stems from mergers with and the acquisitions of local manufacturers in Japan, thus limiting the influence of AmericaCo's business.

In order to achieve the strategic goal of overseas profits comprising 30 per cent of total revenue, the company has three management initiatives according to the 2012 investor relations report of JapanCo group, as set out next:

1   Continue to be a long-term partner for both the customer and the community in three business areas (building automation, advanced automation and the life automation business) using the company's technology and products to provide solutions through the pursuit of human-centred automation.

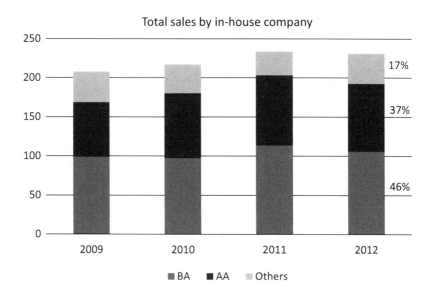

Figure 5.2 Total sales by in-house company (billion JPY)

2 Drive the company's worldwide growth by expanding into new areas and making qualitative changes.
3 Build strong organisations: Never stop learning in order to fully achieve the first two objectives.

Item number two is concerned with the internationalisation of the businesses; given the shrinking domestic market in Japan, international expansion is necessary. Shareholders accept this goal, and the company is struggling to boost overseas revenue since not all the company's subsidiaries have localised their businesses and employees. Interviewees frequently mention the topic of 'localisation', meaning the entire process whereby local employees are hired and trained, with a president being appointed in each subsidiary so that JHQ can delegate its authority to the local management. Although this has not been formally announced as a corporate policy, it is positively promoted and enhanced.

According to the 2012 investor relations report, the current philosophy was based on organisational change undertaken in 2006 when the former CEO was appointed. At that time, the company's symbol and philosophy were revised: the term 'JapanCo' was added to OldJapanCo with a new corporate symbol and the philosophy was revised with the slogan 'human-centered automation'. This slogan means that the technologies and products of JapanCo provide new value not merely for the sake of automation itself but for the benefit of people. The new philosophy has four core values that guide the action of JapanCo, namely safety, comfort, fulfilment and contributing to global environmental preservation. Here is part of the corporate philosophy:

> Under 'JapanCo', the Group strives to realize safety, comfort and fulfilment in people's lives and contribute to global environment[al] preservation through "human-centered automation." To realize this,
>
> - We create value together with customers at their site.
> - We pursue our unique value based on the idea of [being] "human-centered."
> - We think towards the future and act progressively.

These values are created by providing product lines for building and automation companies.

Although it is more than a decade since the dissolution of the alliance, the strong influence of AmericaCo remains. Given the high dependency on AmericaCo, a Japanese VP in JUSA described how JapanCo had a highly conservative culture that did not encourage its employees to develop business themselves. He pointed out how '[JapanCo] [had] never created [a] market on its own . . . the alliance of AmericaCo markets were already there and it [the company] provided mass produced products due to the demand of AmericaCo'. The great dependency on AmericaCo in the past in terms of international sales and marketing implicitly constrained the business development of JapanCo. This outcome, therefore, greatly influences the constellations of logics across the subsidiaries because of their relevance to AmericaCo.

5.2.2.2 Overseas subsidiaries management

In total, there are 12 overseas subsidiaries in JapanCo. Most subsidiaries are in the Asian region and only two are outside this area, these being located in Europe (EU) and the Americas. The largest revenue within the subsidiaries comes from China, where there is a joint venture business with a Chinese manufacturer. Here, the functions are sales, marketing and manufacturing. JTHAI and JTAIW are similar in terms of their sizes and areas of business although both have a different customer base. JTHAI has most of its customers in Japan while JTAIW has local customers. The profiles of all of the subsidiaries are provided in Table 5.3.

To manage the overseas subsidiaries, the International Business Development (IBD) department was formed. This department has five staff members and mainly coordinates financial 'numbers' rather formulating and managing business strategies. The IBD department does not have the authority to manage its businesses, but in-house companies do have the authority to manage their business in the overseas subsidiaries. Here, in-house companies in JHQ have the central authority to set up and manage sales goals and to control the staffing of Japanese expatriates in overseas subsidiaries as well as product pricing, product development and marketing on a global scale. Thus, the in-house company system influences the sales goal-setting process enormously. Under each company, there are sales and marketing departments divided by region to support the subsidiaries. The organisational chart is attached in Figure 5.4.

All of the subsidiaries, except for JUSA, are highly dependent on the management resources of JapanCo's headquarters (JHQ) in Japan because almost all the corporate functions of AA and BA are centralised in JHQ. These functions constitute production, research and development, the global marketing strategy, service and maintenance, while the overseas subsidiaries largely function as sales offices with service functions. There is one exception, however, since JUSA has a manufacturing function and maintains a small factory (it also acquired a local gas metre manufacturer in 2012). JHQ adopted an in-house company system composed of the AA and BA companies; both have independent lines of products and both are managed separately. They do, however, occasionally share the same customers and, in the cases of JTHAI and JUSA where both divisions exist, may sometimes compete for the same customers in terms of orders. JHQ now controls both AA and BA in the subsidiaries.

The sales goals, expatriates and available products in all of the subsidiaries are largely negotiated and determined by the in-house companies in JHQ through IBD. Specifically, annual sales targets are set up as a manifestion of the managers' 'guts' and distributed to each overseas subsidiary without examining their feasibility from interviews. For example, if the Asian region as a whole grew sales by 15 per cent in one year, each of the overseas subsidiaries in Asia would

Table 5.3 Profiles of all the subsidiaries (100 million JPY)

	JapanCo China	JapanCo Korea	JapanCo JTHAI (Thailand)	JTAIW (Taiwan)	JapanCo Indonesia	JUSA (North America)	JapanCo Singapore	JEU (Europe)	JapanCo Philippines	JapanCo Malaysia	JapanCo Vietnam	JapanCo India
Revenue (2011)	100	30	17	18	12	14	11	8	3	5	2	0
Revenue (2012)	117	34	24	19	15	14	13	7	5	4	2	2
# of employees	793	107	136	80	91	77	62	12	49	68	37	22
% of revenue by Japanese customers	30%	10%	80%	30%	10%	15%	10%	0%	20%	20%	30%	30%

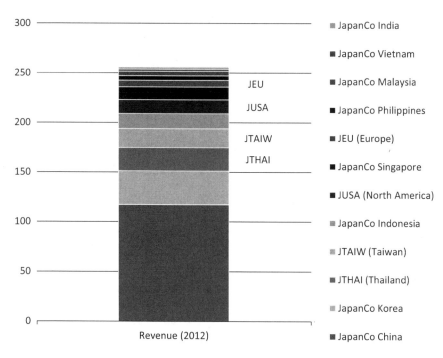

Figure 5.3 Sales volume by subsidiaries (million JPY)

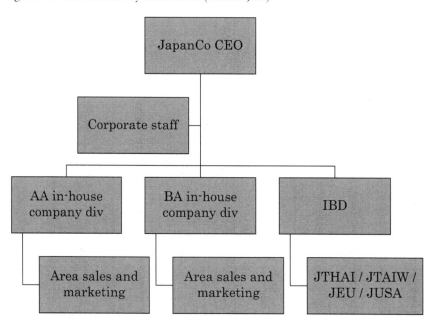

Figure 5.4 The organisational chart of JapanCo

be likely to be allocated a sales increase, this being 15 per cent or more in the next year regardless of whether the revenue of a subsidiary in Asia increased in the initial year. This sales target was provided by JHQ, although some heads of the overseas subsidiaries argued that this sales target was unreasonable and irrational.

The job titles of individual actors in all of the subsidiaries are summarised in Table 5.4:

Table 5.4 The job titles and their descriptions in JapanCo group

Titles	Descriptions
President /Managing director (MD)	Represents the president of each subsidiary
Director /Vice-President (VP)	Responsible for the profits and losses of a business
Manager	Responsible for the profits and losses of a limited business
Non-managerial employees	Those who do not have titles above managers; most are local employees
Japanese expatriates	Expatriates from the Japanese headquarters (JHQ)
Local employees	Those who were recruited in a given location outside Japan

There is always either a Japanese president or a vice-president, with the exception of JapanCo in Indonesia and China, since these businesses are managed as joint ventures. In the selected subsidiaries in the case studies, the president in JUSA is an American, but the others are Japanese.

Japanese expatriates play a central role in communicating with JHQ from each subsidiary although localisation is informally promoted. 'Localisation'

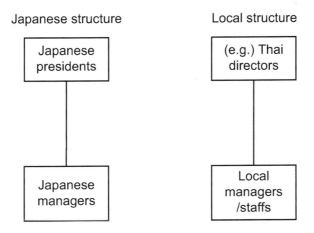

Figure 5.5 The organisational structures between Japanese and locals

refers to a process whereby local employees, not Japanese expatriates, manage local businesses. In practice, however, a group of Japanese expatriates is structurally created and maintained by JHQ. Each in-house company – AA and BA in JHQ – dispatches the next Japanese expatriates, while finally evaluating and approving the performance of their current expatriates, especially the president or vice-president. The performance of the Japanese expatriate manager is normally reviewed by its president, who is most likely to be Japanese. Here, the bonuses and salaries of all the expatriates are linked to their respective performances in JapanCo as a whole group and are not determined by the respective subsidiaries. In other words, the HR system of the Japanese expatriates is free from its business performance. Conversely, for local employees, their performance, salary and bonus are set, evaluated and approved in a given subsidiary. Therefore, although Japanese expatriates are in the same organisational chart with local employees, there are two invisible structures that assess and evaluate managers and staff, these being either Japanese or composed of local employees.

This structural division between Japanese and locals has partially been identified as being composed of informal groups within Japanese MNCs' subsidiaries (see Kopp, 1999; Elger and Smith, 2005). Nonetheless, this division is structurally reinforced in JapanCo (see 8.2). For Japanese expatriates, regardless of their title, their bonus and salary are separated from performance and that of their subsidiaries, being connected instead to the overall performance of JapanCo group. Thus, all Japanese expatriate managers are controlled and managed by a top Japanese president and it is not important if they are above or below their local president, directors, or managers.

There is an annual performance appraisal for Japanese and local employees. Essentially, the Japanese are evaluated by the top-ranked Japanese expatriate and the local employees by the local managers. Japanese expatriates are evaluated by the first direct manager, and then by the department in JHQ from which they were originally dispatched. There is no coherent evaluation or HRM system specifically for Japanese expatriates because the responsible department finally evaluates and approves their performance. According to most Japanese expatriates, the problem is that Japanese expatriates are evaluated by JHQ in such a way that they are compared to other Japanese employees working in Japan and not with other expatriates in other subsidiaries. This comparison leads to an evaluation of Japanese expatriates separately from the performance of their respective subsidiaries, and causes structural and mental separation between the Japanese expatriates and the local employees. When asked about the roles of Japanese expatriates, one local Thai employee stated 'well, [Japanese expatriates] are different [from Thais]'. Moreover, even the American president in JUSA asserted 'I am not like [the Japanese expatriate VP] or like an expatriate from Japan'. This separated evaluation applies to all Japanese expatriates across the subsidiaries of JapanCo group in Asia, Europe and North America.

5.3 The tales of subsidiaries in Asia and the West

5.3.1 Overview of the four subsidiaries

The four subsidiaries selected are: JapanCo in Thailand (JTHAI), JTAIW in Taiwan, JEU in Europe and JUSA in the United States. These cases help to illuminate the cultural meanings of practices through the constellations of logics. Each subsidiary has different features that can affect these constellations of logics. These features are the customer bases, the functions and the organisational identity that they attribute to their subsidiaries as shown in Table 5.5.

At first glance, this table appear to show a simple picture of norms within the subsidiaries. That is, the more Japanese customers there are, the more Japanese norms there are. In JTHAI, the interviewees tend to identify themselves as belonging to 'a Japanese company' and alongside the notion of a Japanese norm, some Thais describe themselves by stating 'we are family . . . in a typical Japanese company'. This company is entirely dependent on JHQ in terms of R&D and manufacturing. In JUSA, however, the interviewees tend to identify themselves as belonging to an American company by quickly answering, 'Oh boy, it's an American company'. Here, the company is less dependent on JHQ than the previous company, and few respondents use the word 'family'. JEU is similar to JUSA, although it is more dependent on JHQ and has a mixed identity, with Japanese and European employees. Situated in between JTHAI and JUSA, JTAIW is shifting from being a Japanese company to being a local one.

These features, however, do not mean that a customer base at each subsidiary determines the actors' cultural interpretations in respect to, for example, the family norm. Nor do they mean that all of the actors in JTHAI, for example, interpret practices through a Japanese family norm in the same manner. Rather, actors attribute cultural meanings to practices according to geographical contexts in respect to their customers, interests and JHQ. Here is a summary of the subsidiaries.

Table 5.5 The features of four subsidiaries at JapanCo

Features	JTHAI (Thailand)	JTAIW (Taiwan)	JUSA (USA)	JEU (EU)
Customer base (its % of revenue)	Japanese customers (70%)	Taiwanese and Chinese customers (70%)	American customers (90%)	AmericaCo and European customers (100%)
Functions	Sales, marketing, service and corporate	Sales, marketing, service and corporate	Sales, marketing, service, manufacturing, R&D and corporate	Sales, marketing and corporate
Organisational identity	Japanese company	Japanese company	American company	Mixed (Japanese and European)

Table 5.6 Detailed profiles of JapanCo and subsidiaries

Items	JapanCo group (JHQ)	JTHAI (Thailand)	JTAIW (Taiwan) (JTAI)	JEU (EU)	JUSA (USA)
Revenue (2012)	200 billion yen	2 billion yen	2 billion yen	70 million yen	1 billion yen
# of employees	5,200	158	56	12	45
# of branch offices	12	2	2	1	3
Ownership	Japanese institutional investors	Owned by JapanCo group	Owned by JapanCo group	Owned by JapanCo group	Owned by JapanCo group
Length of operation	107 years	18 years	13 years	13 years	14 years
Type of business	Automation(A), Building(B), and other in-house companies	A and B in-house companies	A and B in-house companies	A in-house companies	A in-house companies
Ratio of local customers	100%	40%	70%	100%	85%

In the subsequent subsections, some of the features of the four subsidiaries that are likely to be associated with constellations of logics are described: their collective identities, customer base, organisational structure, artefacts and office layout.

5.3.2 Collective identifies of the four subsidiaries

The collective identities of the four subsidiaries vary from 'a Japanese company' to 'an American company' and 'a mixture of Japanese and European'. JTHAI was characterised as 'a typical Japanese company' by all of the interviewees, presumably because of its high reliance on Japanese customers. A Thai HR manager commenting about JTHAI declared, 'I think that JTHAI is not different from other Japanese companies.' Other Thais also expressed the view that JTHAI was a Japanese company, referring to the Japanese presidents and expatriates in management positions. In fact, the company does adopt typical Japanese management practices, such as those of harmony, seniority, management by waking around, an open-door policy and intense socialisation. In addition, Theravada, a school of Buddhism, is influential on the behaviour of the Thai employees.

Similarly, JTAIW tends to be identified as a Japanese company. A Taiwanese manager pointed out how all of the presidents have been Japanese expatriates from either AA or BA companies in JHQ. Another manager emphasised that there were no sales incentives, but some form of seniority did exist. Meanwhile, a Taiwanese director highlighted the business procedure as a reason for the Japanese qualities of the company. Considering that Taiwanese and Chinese customers are increasingly more important than Japanese ones, a Japanese MD asserted that 'we are now in the process of localisation', meaning a change from being a Japanese company to being a local Taiwanese one.

By contrast, JUSA and JEU are closer to being a local corporation. In JUSA, many informants characterise themselves as 'an American company', in the sense that the customer base is American and the company has an American president, although some Japanese characteristics remain in the operational department. One American director, when asked whether JUSA was Japanese or American, asserted: 'Oh, boy! It's an American company'. To justify this statement, he referred to the existence of an American president and VP, many American customers and American salespeople motivated by high sales incentives. All of the businesses here are under AA's control and thus the Japanese VP is dispatched from AA in JHQ.

JEU is identified by European employees as a mixed Japanese and European company. A Belgian director, when asked if JEU was Japanese or European, explained that it was:

> a bit of a mix of everything I think. Because of the cost, we have to think about the Japanese culture and the Japanese mother company who have as a group, certain rules, certain procedures, a certain way of working, a certain way of thinking, which is different from the European way. And on the other side, yeah, we have to talk to the European customers and our main goal,

main job, is to build the bridge between the knowledge in Japan and the amount of the customers in Europe.

The notion of a mix of Japanese and Europeans is manifest in conflicts within JEU in relation to JHQ and its local customers. JEU has also long dealt with AmericaCo in Europe and other European manufacturers.

In fact, JEU was founded to deal with AmericaCo as both a customer and an alliance partner at that time, and AmericaCo Europe has indeed been one of JEU's largest customers. It was an original equipment manufacturer (OEM) customer, buying and reselling JapanCo's products. Thus, JEU has been reliant on AmericaCo, in contrast to JTHAI, which has relied on incoming Japanese customers.

5.3.3   *Customer bases of the four subsidiaries*

The customer base of the four subsidiaries vary from a majority of Japanese customers in JTHAI to that of local customers in JTAIW, JUSA and JEU. Originally, JTHAI opened as a subsidiary in Thailand in response to requests from Japanese customers. As a Japanese expatriate succinctly explained: '[W]e were taken by the initiative of Japanese customers who wanted to start [an] overseas business in Thailand.' From the time that it opened, the company expanded its business as a Japanese manufacturer starting to enter the Thai market. Figure 5.6 shows total sales by customers.

Currently, JTHAI has two main strategic initiatives: one is to acquire new local customers and the other is to retain existing Japanese customers. The existing Japanese customers are the main source of revenue, providing more than 80 per cent of current sales. The main strategic initiative was to maintain the existing Japanese customer base. These customers were not merely subsidiaries that were 100 per cent owned by Japanese companies but also Japanese joint ventures with local companies. Since Thailand's economic recovery in 2002, and as demand for building Japanese plants in Thailand has grown, JTHAI has continuously expanded. The increase in revenue is now almost 10 per cent more per year and, so far, this has largely been due to an increasing number of incoming Japanese customers. (Its history is attached in the appendix.)

JTAIW is now adopting a localising strategy, which penetrates both the Taiwanese and Chinese customers, both being connected to a number of manufacturing plants in a growing Chinese market. Since 2008, some Japanese customers have started to withdraw their business from Taiwan and others have relocated to China because of the financial crisis. There has, therefore, been a fundamental shift from Japanese customers to local ones. This shift goes along with the increasing importance of the Taiwanese and Chinese customers, who tend to purchase their products in Taiwan but receive them on-site in China. Nowadays, more than half of JTAIW's customers are non-Japanese, typically either Taiwanese or Chinese. See Figure 5.7. (Its history is attached in the appendix.)

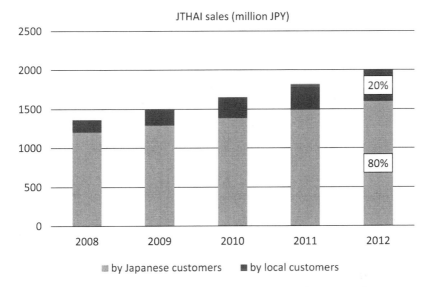

Figure 5.6 JTHAI sales by customers

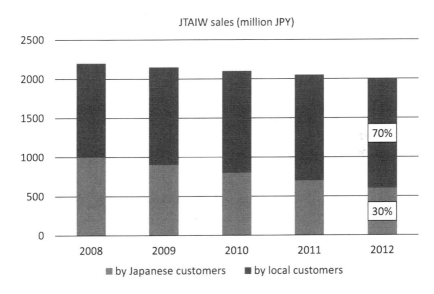

Figure 5.7 JTAIW sales by customers

Unlike JTHAI, both JUSA and JEU are primarily focusing on local customers, American and European manufactures, and relationships with AmericaCo as a customer. Since the termination of the strategic alliance with AmericaCo, JUSA has focused on local American customers. In fact, JUSA has adopted a localised strategy concentrating on local customers in the United States with local employees. Nearly 85 per cent of the revenue comes from local, non-Japanese customers, who are mostly American. In the past five years, however, sales have been flat because of a decline in the semiconductor market. Thus, the main new initiative of JUSA is to develop Japanese as well as American customers. Japanese automotive manufacturers in the United States are the focus because sales activities for the manufacturer were not previously conducted in a proactive manner. Semiconductor equipment manufacturers and shale gas plants are specified as potential American and Japanese customers. Both customers were approached by the American sales team under the Japanese VP's leadership. In particular, shale gas plants are a potential source of business for both American and Japanese manufacturers. When using gas metre products from a newly acquired American company, the Japanese VP aims to develop a shale gas plants market. See Figure 5.8. (Its history is attached in the appendix.)

Similarly, JEU deals with only non-Japanese, European and American customers. JEU is now adopting a localised strategy to acquire new local customers (such as plant engineering companies and electronic manufacturers), by providing solutions that combine industrial parts. JEU used to adopt routine sales activities that provided products for the past alliance partner, AmericaCo, with the latter buying and reselling JapanCo products. The new strategy of the current president, however, aims to formulate solutions and become a solution provider to local customers. This concept should provide solutions by combining existing products as required by customers, rather than simply selling the products. For example, customers might want is to adjust a certain amount of gas or liquid in the plants. In this way, JEU can provide a system to control the gas/liquid amounts in plant manufacturers. This type of strategy is not intended to be decreed by the

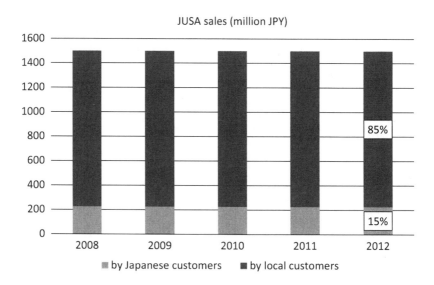

Figure 5.8 JUSA sales by customers

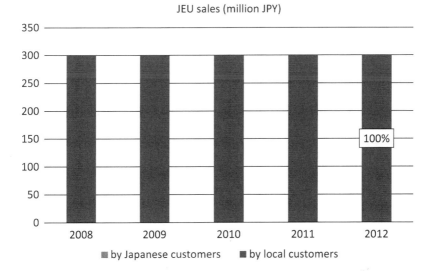

Figure 5.9 JEU sales by customers

Japanese president, but should be formulated together with the local employees. (Its history is attached in the appendix.)

One of the major customers is AmericaCo, which accounts for more than 60 per cent of JEU's revenue. The rest are Western companies from America or Europe, and this focus on local customers requires local expertise. This scenario makes JEU a localised company of JapanCo to an even greater extent, particularly due to interpersonal communication, the way of doing business and the company's norms and beliefs. A particular point of frustration on the part of the local Belgian employees concerns the Japanese way of doing business, such as the procedure of launching and terminating products and services. Employees here asked questions such as: 'Why does JEU bring [a] Japanese way of doing things here in [the] European market. We, Europeans, know more about this market than the Japanese.' See Figure 5.9.

5.3.4 Organisational structures of the four subsidiaries

The organisational structures of the four subsidiaries greatly depend on the business functions in the subsidiaries. All of the subsidiaries, except JUSA, have mainly sales and service functions. Only JUSA has R&D and manufacturing functions.

In JTHAI, the current organisational structure is divided into the same divisions as the headquarters: i.e. two divisions – AA and BA divisions – two additional sales branches that sell the products of both divisions and a corporate department including HRM, IT, accounting and logistics. Figure 5.10 shows the general organisational chart, complete with the number of staff.

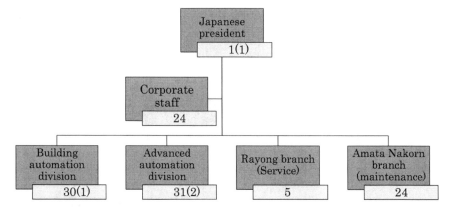

Figure 5.10 The overall organisational chart in JTHAI

There are four Japanese expatriates in total, two in the Advanced Automation division, one in the Building Automation division, with the last one being the president. Temporary visitors from headquarters also come and go on a regular basis. The corporate and sales branches are composed entirely of Thai employees. More recently, for the first time Thai managers have been promoted as directors in JTHAI. This has meant that local Thai directors are in charge of all the local businesses in Thailand. (The historical change in the organisational structure between Japanese expatriates and local employees is shown in Figure 5.11.) The organisational chart of each division is attached in the appendix.

The organisational charts for the Building and Advanced sections where the Japanese are located are as follows.

Similarly, JTAIW has two divisions: AA and BA divisions. Because of the institutionalised rule of localisation, Taiwanese have been appointed to director positions in each division. In the AA division, the director is Taiwanese and all the managers except for one are Taiwanese. In BA, a Taiwanese manager was recently promoted as the deputy director. Figures 5.12 and 5.13 show the organisational charts for both AA and BA divisions. Historically, almost all the MDs are Japanese expatriates. The number of Japanese expatriates is added in parentheses. The organisational chart of each division is attached in the appendix.

JUSA only has the AA division. Unlike the other three subsidiaries, the current president is an American and not an expatriate from JHQ. His main role is not to manage the business but to function as a chief financial officer (CFO) because JUSA had a problem with accounting under the former Japanese presidents. Here, the Japanese expatriate was appointed as vice-president and communicated with JHQ. In practice, the Japanese vice-president tends to play the role of the president and is expected to initiate business and communicate with JHQ (see Figures 5.14 and 5.15).

In the sales and marketing division, the Japanese vice-president is an acting director who formally manages the development of both Japanese and American

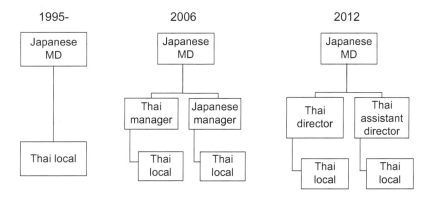

Figure 5.11 Historical change of organisational structure in JTHAI 1995

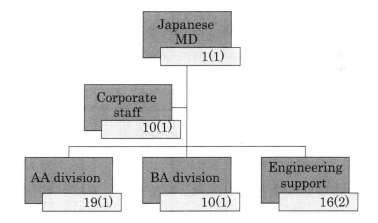

Figure 5.12 The organisational chart of JTAIW

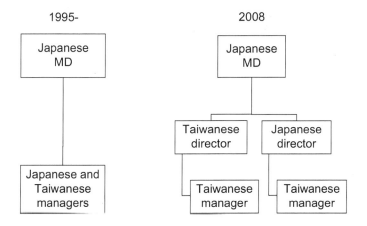

Figure 5.13 Historical change of organisational structure in JTAIW

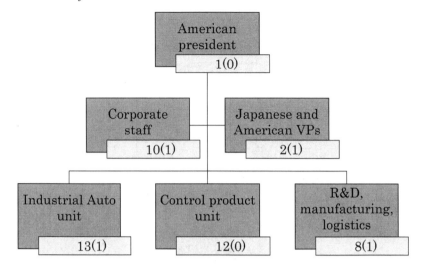

Figure 5.14 The overall organisational chart of JUSA

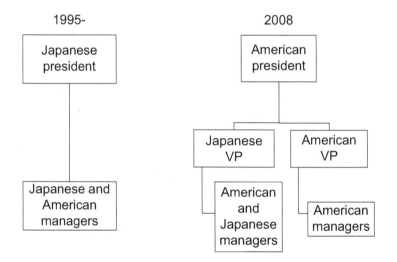

Figure 5.15 Historical change of organisational structure in JUSA 1995

customers. There are Japanese expatriate salespeople who are mainly responsible for Japanese automotive manufacturers in the United States. The rest of the American sales managers and staff are responsible for American customers. In 2008, the current American president was appointed.

JEU also only has an AA division. The total number of employees in JEU is now 12. The MD is a Japanese expatriate, and another two Japanese expatriates work in Germany as temporary engineers. Hence, the organisational structure in JEU is simple: the Japanese president manages all of the local employees. The office of JEU is composed of a main office in Belgium and a sub-office in

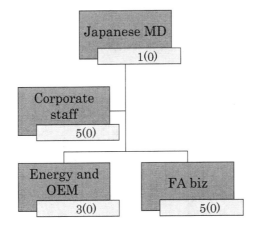

Figure 5.16 The organisational chart of JEU

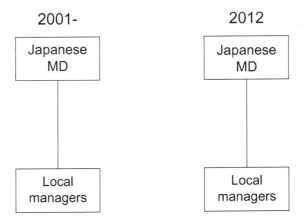

Figure 5.17 The historical changes in the organisational structure in JEU 2001

Germany. The organisational structure is clearly defined by the individual job descriptions. There is a small branch office in Germany, with four employees. The current and former MD are all Japanese expatriates (see Figures 5.16 and 5.17).

5.3.5 Artefacts and office layouts of the four subsidiaries

The artefacts and office layouts also vary according to the customer base and the businesses of each subsidiary. In JTHAI, as with JHQ, non-managerial members tend to share the same long desk in sales divisions, and there are no partitions except for the corporate staff members. This resembles a typical Japanese company office in Japan, and the engineers do not have their own space or desk because they often stay on the customers' sites. Only the Japanese MD has a private room, while the managers have their own desks and spaces, but without partitions. Its office layout is shown in Figure 5.18.

By contrast, in JTAIW, the office layout is different from that of JHQ, where every non-managerial employee shares the same desk. At JTAIW, all of the employees have their own desk and space separated by partitions. Only the Japanese MD and two members in the finance department have a private room for security reasons since they deal with personal information, such as salaries and legal information. Its office layout is shown in Figure 5.19.

Unlike JHQ and JTHAI, the office layout in JUSA is spacious and all of the management members, such as the president and VPs, have a private room.

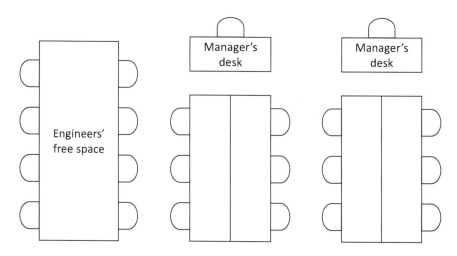

Figure 5.18 The office layout of JTHAI

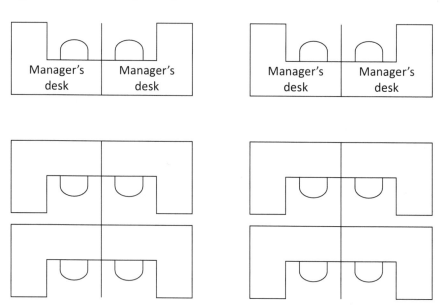

Figure 5.19 The office layout of JTAIW

The other members also have their own desks and spaces. There are partitions between the desks that are low enough for them to see each other and a space in front of the desks in the office in Phoenix where there is a weekly quality control meeting. Its office layout is shown in Figure 5.20.

Similarly, the office layout in JEU is not like that of JHQ where everybody shares a long desk. Rather, each member has his or her own desk while sharing the same room. Only the Japanese MD and the HR manager have a private room. The office is spacious and its members can easily talk to each other. Its office layout is shown in Figure 5.21.

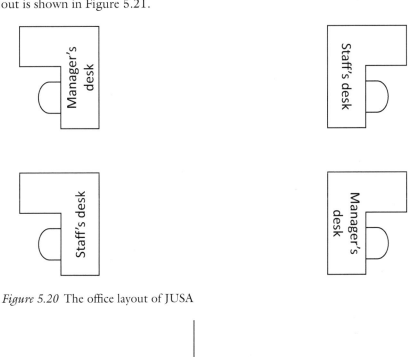

Figure 5.20 The office layout of JUSA

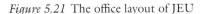

Figure 5.21 The office layout of JEU

5.4 Conclusion

This chapter has sought to provide relevant background to interpret the remaining empirical chapters. With the alliance partner of AmericaCo, JapanCo is characterised as a unique and atypical Japanese corporation, possibly causing complex cultural meanings in practices through varied constellations of logics. Here, two major elements influencing the cultural interpretations of each subsidiary in terms of collective identities are provided: the main type of customers locally and the dependence on JHQ. Identified as 'a typical Japanese company', JTHAI seems to be associated with Japanese management practices according to a large Japanese customer base. It also depends on JHQ in terms of their products and services. By contrast, JUSA and JEU have a strong influence from AmericaCo and their local customers, thereby being identified as 'an American company' and 'a mixture of Japanese and European company' by their local employees. JTAIW is facing a change in its customer base from Japanese to non-Japanese, such as Taiwanese and Chinese, yet still identifies as a Japanese company. Furthermore, an examination was also made of the dependence on the resources of JHQ where research and development functions are concentrated. In particularly, JUSA is relatively independent from JHQ because of its manufacturing and R&D functions while the others, such as JTHAI, JTAIW and JEU, rely on manufacturing and R&D resources in JHQ. These subsidiaries have to communicate frequently with JHQ to enquire about and negotiate on prices, delivery and the quality of the products.

Nevertheless, this does not mean that these features of the subsidiaries determine the actors' cultural meanings in respect to practices. Rather, it is a feature that generates complex cultural interpretations of practice through the constellations of logics that will be explored Chapters 6, 7 and 8.

6 *Ongaeshi* as a return for favour to organisations

Customer development

6.1 Introduction

This chapter covers how the practices of customer development are culturally interpreted through cooperative relationships among logics. It is organised into three sections. First, the context of the dominant Japanese culture is reviewed. Second, *oyabun, kobun, ongaeshi* and family relationships in Japanese are discussed. Finally, Thai Theravada Buddhism is described. In a concluding section, two findings, with a related discussion, are offered: Japanese family and Thai Theravada Buddhism logics are interpreted showing that culturally enacted logics can be amplified in a cooperative manner.

6.2 Collective efforts to develop Japanese customers

Japanese customer development has long been recognised as a collective effort in JapanCo's international development. To be exact, JapanCo has long followed Japanese customers going abroad, rather than initiating its internationalisation by itself. The Japanese managing director in JTHAI claims that 'we were taken by the initiative of [Japanese] customers who wanted to start overseas businesses'. He critically asserts that the JapanCo group has never formulated and executed an overseas strategy on its own. As a consequence of chasing Japanese customers in Japan, it has, in turn, followed what Japanese customers told them in overseas markets. This heavy dependence on Japanese customers echoes the idea of 'relational embeddedness' in Asia (Collinson and Rugman, 2008) in which the Japanese customers allow 'customer-led new product development'. In particular, this is evident in JTHAI where the main business is to develop the existing and incoming Japanese customers. While JTHAI has developed its business with Japanese customers since its foundation, with Japanese customers comprising more than 70 per cent of its total revenue, JUSA and JTAIW started with a similar intention but now have few Japanese customers. Meanwhile, all of JEU's customers are non-Japanese.

In practice, Japanese expatriates are the primary contacts and play a key role in the selling process: proposing products and services and executing sales projects, for instance, installing valves or air conditioning systems into factories, and closing the sales contracts and collecting receivables. This is mainly because communications with the customer contacts are conducted in Japanese if they are Japanese. A Japanese expatriate manager in JTHAI explains:

> In the projects handled by Japanese managers at [the Japanese] customers, Japanese expatriates are all the contacts for the customers . . . Thais wouldn't get involved in. . . . They would be under our [Japanese] control and told by us to submit this and that quotation . . . [in the projects by Thais] it will be totally reversed . . . they do not consult each other . . . so both of us [Japanese and Thais] do live and let live . . . as a matter of fact, it is meaningless to get Thais involved with Japanese in handling projects so I would rather tell them to do as they are told . . .

This is consistent with how Japanese customer development occurs in JTAIW and JUSA. In most sales jobs, local employees are the 'doers' while the Japanese expatriates are the leaders. This means that Japanese expatriates plan and give orders to local employees about what to do. A Japanese MD in JTHAI quotes how it works in practice:

> before the launch of a project . . . pre-project work design and quotation are work tasks which Japanese at customers are responsible so I will be in charge of these tasks . . . then, after project acquisition, say let's execute it at site, local employees will take over and implement these projects . . .

So, due to the Japanese customer contacts, the roles of Japanese and local employees are fixed. In practice, Japanese-to-Japanese relations between JapanCo's subsidiaries and Japanese customers in a given location is constantly prioritised in the Japanese customer relationship.

This Japanese-to-Japanese relationship is based on the collective identity of company as family. This relationship allows actors to view Japanese customers as organisational assets, meaning that it needs to be shared and in turn developed with a collective effort as in Japan. Intensive socialisation, seniority and seasonal greetings are identified in developing Japanese customers. For instance, Japanese top management tends to be invited for a greeting by the customer. A Japanese vice-president (VP) mentioned that 'I still make a greeting to Japanese customers here in the United States because I am often invited by them'. All of the Japanese expatriate directors or presidents tend to greet the existing or new Japanese customers in a host country. The Japanese expatriate explained that 'the main aim of the greeting is to gain more sales opportunities from the Japanese customer locally which the Japanese are visiting'. He went on to mention that 'I made a greeting with some Japanese customers and then, got sales opportunities to submit a quotation, which is not yet finalized . . . so everyone makes a visit for greeting Japanese customers locally but not [for American customers]'. All of the customers are not *keiretsu* but the greeting custom still remains even outside Japan, as in JUSA.

Moreover, in JTHAI, this close relationship with Japanese customers enacts Japanese cultural collectivism. There are no individual sales incentives in developing Japanese customers because of aspects of organisational assets. This is remarkably consistent with the sales activities in JHQ where all Japanese salespeople are assumed to contribute to team goals and be rewarded by promotion. Although sales quotas are assigned by individual salespeople, salespeople there share the same Japanese corporate customers so they are expected to cooperate together with team members and mentor the inexperienced ones. In line with the same assumption, the Japanese MD in JTAIW assumes that Japanese customer development itself should be, and actually is, treated as an organisational effort. He views sales performance from Japanese customers because of teamwork rather than individual performance. In fact, there is an individual sales incentive programme but only for local salespeople in JUSA and JEU, where it is a common business practice, but not in JTHAI and JTAIW. In addition, salespeople, when developing Japanese customers, are expected to have technological expertise and knowledge, as in Japan. Thus, the title of local Thai salespeople in JTHAI, for example, is not just salesperson but sales engineer (SE) in order for them to deal with Japanese customers.

The fact that there are surrounding Japanese players, Japanese customers, Japanese expatriates opens up a cultural space to be filled with Japanese family and collectivism, as Kondo (1990) articulate. Japanese customer development is conducted through the actors' cultural interpretations of Japanese family and other logics: market, corporation and religion as reviewed in a next few subsections.

6.3 Dealing with Japanese customers through Japanese family logic

The Japanese family-like relationship is supported by a clanship in the corporation, rather than the blood relationship normally assumed in a family. This notion of family is shown in the interviews with Thai sales managers in JTHAI. A Thai sales manager describes his sales force as a family by saying that 'we are family', as Kondo articulates (1990). He and his subordinates often go out together, have lunches and dinners together, even go on company and team trips together. He treats his men as his kids and tries constantly to advise them formally and informally. Other managers also use the word 'family' as an expression for their salesforces. This concept of family is deeply associated with the Japanese cultural version of family when they develop Japanese customers.

Another Thai manager, who was brought up in Japan and speaks fluent Japanese, raises the importance of family, which possibly stems from his relationship with Japanese customers. In actual interview, he called his subordinates kids. He went on to point out that this notion of family might transpose from Japanese customers to his sales force. He stated:

> Given a generation gap [between the customer contacts and his subordinates], the contacts at customers whom I have dealt with are promoted to

become directors so *"Ko"* [my kids in English] whom I took to customers tend to communicate with the same job titles within [Japanese] customers organizations. I could talk to anyone, but my subordinates neither directly talk to a director nor are allowed to talk by him. There is a seniority based [social] order [within the Japanese customers' organizations]. My subordinates instruct their men in the same way [as I do].

Treating subordinates as *ko* ('kids'), he views managing people as nurturing young subordinates much like his kids. This paternalism is the Japanese version of the family where the older has to care for the younger. It also means that Japanese family members in the corporation are ranked by seniority, rather than by their performance; Bhappu (2000) states that 'achievement is second to trust' in Japanese organisations. The seniority here is based on a Japanese father and child relationship transposed into Japanese customer organisations. In order for the Thai manager to communicate effectively with the contacts in Japanese customer organisations, he utilises the concept of Japanese seniority in his sales force. He expects and teaches his *ko* to do the same as he maintains the seniority. This seniority of the family is manifested in Japanese business organisations (the corporation logic) for gaining economic benefits (the market logic).

Furthermore, this father and child relationship is strongly implied between Thai managers and their Thai subordinates. At first sight, the Japanese family seems to be legitimised by full 'unconditional loyalty' just as the Western family means a child's complete dependence on his or her father (Thornton et al., 2012). In reference to the *oyabun kobun* relationship, however, a Japanese ritual kinship relationship (e.g. Ishino, 1953), the Thai manager emphasises the concept of family in Japanese as a metaphor when providing practical advice to his subordinates. The subordinate, as a child, should follow advice from, and learn from, the manager, as a father. He describes how to train and instruct his men.

[For subordinates] rather than teamwork unconditional support is necessary. It is from mental to professional support. Like an older brother caring [for] the younger, I need to teach them by visiting the customer sites together. The experienced [the old] need to instruct the inexperienced [the young]. I teach the basics and they follow me, and let them see what '*Oyabun*' [their boss] is doing. I have them see my interaction with [Japanese] customers. They in general would understand what this business is in one year and half, or two years. Yet, they still need to learn more continuously.

He characterises his men as his children who need to copy his behaviours and attitudes as he insists that 'as a child grows, the parents let him watch how they live, so my men should do the same'. Occasionally seizing his chance to teach his children especially in visiting Japanese customers, he tends to tell what is right and wrong in communicating with the Japanese customers. In this sense, parents are always their children's role model. In fact, when I was a salesperson in Japan, I was trained exactly like this. This expression is often used as a typical way of raising the inexperienced salespeople by Japanese managers. The experienced need to take on the role of the father to raise the inexperienced as a young child. This is distinctive in the sense that this Japanese family norm exists within a corporation. By contrast, the Western family primarily concerns a blood relationship, thus caring for only the direct family.

This Japanese family strongly implies 'reciprocity and obligation' (Bhappu, 2000; Kondo, 1990) between a father and his children. It means that the relationship between a father and his child is expected to be legitimised through reciprocal obligation. In addition to on-the-job training, the Thai manager regularly facilitates study groups within his department as part of sales training. In the study group, the inexperienced salesperson can study the JapanCo product lines. This study usually takes place once a week during non-working hours – non-payable hours, in other words. He emphasises the burden on his children by asserting that 'each member should study the products on his own': it is an obligation of his children as responsible family members. He exemplifies that 'for instance, this week, my subordinate is ordered to study the heat source system, and he studies this and becomes a teacher in this study group . . . normally, we need to deal with another new job when we do a topic by half'. This attitude strongly manifests not the Western family but the Japanese family norm where the family is based on reciprocity and obligation.

Moreover, this Japanese family relationship is also distinct from the Western family in terms of *ongaeshi*, which means repayment to someone to whom one thinks one owes a lot. *Ongaeshi* is the Japanese word that describes how children, once they have become an adult, need to repay (*gaeshi*) their parents in exchange for having received the favour of being nurtured (*on*). Bhappu (2000) considers this concept as the basis of the Japanese family relationship. Through Japanese customer development, the Japanese vice-president in JUSA states that his ultimate goal is not promotion or a salary raise. What motivates him to grow drastically the business of JUSA is to conduct *ongaeshi* by repaying those who had taught and trained him since he joined JapanCo. He asserts:

> I would not be working here if I want to make much money . . . I could not make much money here . . . I could change a job and there is a plenty outside of JapanCo, and actually many job opportunities came to me . . . but even if I change the job, I'm not sure that I would continue to have fun in the job as I do . . . so my goal is to grow the business of JTHAI, not to change a job for a higher salary . . . I have owed a lot to [JapanCo] and many olds . . . indeed [JapanCo] is not a great prestigious company but I could not find myself outside here . . .

Here, he denies that he is motivated by a higher salary or promotion. His motivation is to grow the business based on repaying JapanCo group, or *ongaeshi*. This moment is when he repays what he believes he owes: a sense of being trained and nurtured. So he concludes that 'it is absolute that I do achieve good economic results in order to respect those to whom I have owned'.

Thus, for him, to grow the business of JUSA is not the sole purpose of his business but is simply his obligation in exchange for what he has received. Developing the American market is simply one approach of conducting *ongaeshi*. He continues to explain what *ongaeshi* means to him:

> It's not only America, America is just a result of me being transferred, and then I just came here by chance. . . . It's simply because I have owed a lot to JapanCo in Japan, and JapanCo asked me to expand the business of JUSA, therefore, it is imperative for me to repay by growing the business, thereby doing "*Ongaeshi*".

This American market development is purely economic activity while encouraged by family obligation because he feels *ongaeshi* in Japanese. *Ongaeshi* originally stems from the family relationship between parents and their child. Similarly, there is another Japanese expatriate manager who continues to work at JUSA due to the advice from his senior, *senpai*. He is trying to keep the words of the seniors who used to advise him and even protect him within JapanCo from being treated in an irrational manner, such as being relocated or fired. He still keeps the words that he was told to 'put the customer needs first whenever you cannot decide'. He was also advised to 'be patient and continue to stay at JapanCo' when he wanted to resign before. The family relationship with his seniors still remains and directs local customer development.

This indicates actors' cultural interpretation of Japanese family logic, which is somewhat distinctive from the Western family logic based on unconditional loyalty. Japanese expatriates incline to repay by increasing economic results while feeling this obligation for the seniors who cared them. This also develops the reciprocity and obligation relationship based on *ko* and *on* as Kondo (1990) and Bhappu (2000) assert. A series of Japanese management scholars, mainly non-Japanese, fail to illuminate these cultural interpretations of the market logic because they lack 'area knowledge', as Elger and Smith (2005) point out.

6.4 Gaining religious merits in sales follow-up

This family norm is strongly manifested among the Thai salesforces, rather than Japanese expatriates. In fact, none of Japanese expatriates in JTHAI expressed themselves by saying that 'we are family' as the Thai managers do. The Japanese MD, when asked whether he thinks of JTHAI as family was dead set against the concept of family. He said that 'for me, this is not "family" but a professional workplace. Family sounds very light-hearted. I could not take it easy'. Another Japanese expatriate manager interprets Japanese 'family' among Thai employees differently. He argues for Theravada Buddhism by stating:

> . . . everybody here gets along with each other . . . and tends to give a hand to inexperienced employees and others . . . there is probably Theravada Buddhism behind these behaviours . . .

He asserts that for the Thai, it is the religion logic of Theravada Buddhism that is activated rather than the family logic. He points out the importance of religious merit in Theravada Buddhism for the Thai employees: helping others, showing benevolence and forgiving the mistakes of others. Indeed, Theravada Buddhism is the dominant religion in Thailand, observed by about 95 per cent of the citizens (Atmiyanandana and Lawler, 2003). The concept of Japanese family with obligation and reciprocity may be emphasised through Theravada Buddhism, where the ultimate purpose is to gain religious merit through mundane jobs.

Similarly, another Japanese expatriate casts doubt on this family that the Thais always mention, although it is admired by other Japanese expatriates. Rather, he calls these practices, which are conducted by the Thai manager and his subordinates, as 'quasi-Japanese management practices' with some individualism. He means that these practices, while superficially similar to Japanese practices, are somehow 'Thai' Japanese practices influenced by Theravada Buddhism, which promotes the practices of helping others for religious merit. He adds that gaining religious merit, or *tam bun* in Thai, which is central to the Thai people, can be achieved not only by making a donation but also by forgiving and helping others in order for them to achieve a good 'next life', as Atmiyanandana and Lawler (2003) explain. The study group, for instance, can also be interpreted not as maintaining the Japanese family norm but as gaining religious merits. It is neither organised nor ordered by the Japanese expatriates but purely volunteered by the Thai manager. All of the other Thai managers proactively provide on-the-job training for sales, even after working hours. This on-the-job training is also not assigned as a job or ordered by the Japanese expatriates. In the same way, at social events, the person with the highest position tends to be the one to pay all the bills to gain religious merit (see 7.4.1). The Japanese expatriate exemplifies this case as a typical Japanese management practice among Thai local employees, stating that '[Thais] get along with each other and tend to help each other.' He admires that Thai employees are doing good with this practice. These may superficially look like 'a Japanised subsidiary', as a Japanese expatriate mentioned, yet it is not Japanese but in some sense the Thai religion. In addition, although both Japanese and Thai nations are collectivistic societies, family from the Thai point of view seems to be influenced by religious aspects since the Thai behaviour of gaining religious merit is based on individual efforts.

This view becomes evident in sales follow-up. For instance, there was a large sales opportunity from a customer. A Thai salesperson was expected to submit a quotation by the deadline but did not prepare until the day before. As a result, the opportunity was lost. The only person who got angry over the sales loss and closely questioned the salesperson was a Japanese expatriate. In this case, the Japanese expatriates became upset over lost sales and yelled at local Thai salesperson. Thai directors, however, reacted differently. They tended to view a lost sale as an opportunity to gain Theravada Buddhism merits. In losing sales opportunities, they try to gain religious merits by resigning to their mistakes. According to the Japanese expatriate, Thai managers or directors showed no reaction over this incident. He stated that 'well, none of the Thai managers blamed the salesperson for losing the sales opportunity . . . they were just saying *mai pen rai* ('never mind') . . . this is incredible'. A Japanese expatriate suspected that behind this incident is the concept of gaining a religious merit, or *tam bun*. According to him, not only making a donation but also forgiving and helping others are the means to make religious merits in Theravada Buddhism. In other words, forgiving and helping others are not for business purposes such as expanding the business and increasing the revenue but for gaining one's own religious merit. This religious merit in Theravada Buddhism is reflected in an ideal Thai leader helping and forgiving (Atmiyanandana and Lawler, 2003).

This Japanese expatriate interprets the religious merit as a guiding principle for Thai people in business as well as in daily life. This principle is possibly related to the ultimate interest for Thais, which is to gain religious merit to have a better next life by being born into a wealthy family (Atmiyanandana and Lawler, 2003). When comparing this principle with Japanese behaviours, he shared his interpretation of the Thais:

> They [Thais] would not scold or call you an idiot but would treat you really well. This is expected in order to make them great men; men of religious virtue. I imagine that, even if one makes a mistake, they would still forgive him in order to be able to go to Sukhavati [Land of Bliss]. I am wondering if they think of it this way. I have recently been considering this. Neither have they investigated into the cause [of lost sales] nor have they made a critical movement in others [sales].

In actual work practices, this resignation is highly likely to bring about another economically irrational result in sales activities because it does not allow any investigation into what causes lost opportunities and therefore learning from a mistake. For the Thais, it is a passive action to gain a religious merit while for the Japanese, it results in 'no learning curve'. One's current status is a consequence of one's prior life; thereby the Thais continue to revise their possible future status by seeking to gain religious merits.

The religious norm is strongly implicated in the tendency to be benevolent to others although this is not clearly articulated by the local Thai employees. A local Thai director responded to the question regarding how to deal with salespeople who are losing sales opportunities. Unlike the Japanese president, he pointed out that applying pressure on sales itself is not right. He claimed:

> We [Thais] do not give much pressure by asking why, why and why to the sales managers. I just try to help them explain the situation. My style is different from that of the [Japanese] president who is always asking why, why and why.

It is true that, due to the importance of forgiveness, he tends not to investigate, nor be investigated, about the cause. Religious norms seem to be implicit among Thai employees. In the interviews, he clearly denies the existence of Theravada

Buddhism in the workplace when asked whether Theravada Buddhism may or may not influence Thai behaviours. Similarly, there are some Thai employees, when developing local customers, who insist on sales incentives for individual sales performance. They often ask Japanese expatriates, 'Why do we need to acquire and develop new local customers . . . since we have enough Japanese customers.' They often insist on an increase in salary by taking on difficult tasks, such as acquiring local customers. However, the fact that they end up smiling or being quiet in the face of lost sales opportunities tends to be understood by the Japanese as a reflection of Thai religious beliefs. This forgiveness and avoidance of anger is accommodated not only by the cultural custom but also by Theravada Buddhism, which encourages Thais to gain religious merits such as by being generous, by forgiving others and by helping others.

6.5 Discussion and conclusion

This chapter has sought to understand how the practices of customer development are culturally interpreted through cooperative relationships among logics. Two main findings are identified in this chapter: Japanese family and Thai Theravada Buddhism logic, which are culturally interpreted, culturally enacted logics that can be amplified in a cooperative manner.

The first finding is that the Japanese family logic and Thai Theravada Buddhism are culturally interpreted and enacted according to their national cultures. The distinctions are threefold. The concept of the Japanese family is not the same as that of the Western family. The Japanese family is governed by reciprocal *ko* and *on* relationships, rather than the unconditional loyalty that legitimates the Western family (Thornton et al., 2012). This view originates from the importance of the reproduction of family members as Friedland and Alford (1991) state. This Western family logic seems to be consistent with Western family firms (e.g. Karra et al., 2006). What legitimises the Japanese family, however, is reciprocity and obligation based on the Japanese notion of family. *Oyabun kobun* and *senpai* are expressed as a burden of Japanese family members: *ongaeshi*, repayment to those to whom one owes a debt, especially in the context of a child or subordinate who is obligated to return the favour to parents or seniors for the nurturing they offered. The Japanese vice-president in JUSA is originally motivated to return the favour to *senpai*, the senior to whom he thinks he owes a debt (see 6.3). For him, it is common sense to return the favour by generating profits. Then, he further interprets a demand for *ongaeshi* based on Japanese family logic in the context of a corporation. This meaning of family is also influenced by the collectivistic nature of Japanese society (Hofstede, 2010). It has little to do with unconditional loyalty as such, prioritising more 'reciprocity and obligation rather than obedience (Bhappu, 2000)'. It is also not consistent with the parental altruism that can be manifested in Western family firms (e.g. Karra et al., 2006; Nordqvist and Melin, 2010).

Next, each meaning of 'family' in Japan and the West entails a different scope of family members. The Japanese family means an expanded concept of family including non-blood relationships (Bhappu, 2000), while the Western family usually means direct blood relationship in a nuclear family. It even includes its subordinates as family members by saying that 'we are family'. A body of literature about family firms tends to assume blood relations for the enactment of family logic in terms of their ownership and structure (Chung and Luo, 2008; Thornton et al., 2012). The family in Japan, however, includes the non-blood relationship; as Kondo (1990) asserts, *ie* in Japan should not be treated just as a kinship based on biological blood relations but is 'best understood as [a] corporate group that holds property (for example, land, a reputation, an art or "cultural capital") in perpetuity' (Kondo (1990). This view is also connected to the national culture: in Japan's collectivistic society, 'people "in groups" that take care of them in exchange for loyalty' while in an individualistic society, 'people are supposed to look after themselves and their direct "family" only' (Hofstede, 2010).

Finally, Thai Theravada Buddhism logics are also culturally interpreted. In contrast to Mahayana Buddhism, Theravada Buddhism enables actors to gain religious merits in the form of outward signs during their daily lives (Atmiyanandana and Lawler, 2003). The Thai Theravada Buddhism logic is not consistent with the meanings of Western logics as put forward by Thornton et al. (2012). A leader in Theravada Buddhism is expected to be a benevolent father. This view contrasts with a religion logic based on Christianity, governed by 'sacredness' (Thornton et al., 2012). Although Thornton et al. (2012) utilised a more universal religious logic, it is still based on a fundamentally Christian view of religion, which may not be easily transferred to the Asian context. This Theravada Buddhism version of the religion logic is deeply embedded in Thai society as a logic rooted in a national context as its 'geographical community' (Lounsbury, 2007). Both Japanese 'family' and Thai Theravada Buddhism once again highlight the limitations of the current Western institutional logics perspective, eventually implying that these perspectives cannot be universally applied.

The second finding is that culturally enacted logics can be amplified in a cooperative manner. This finding directly elaborates on the presupposition of amplification itself (Greenwood et al., 2010; 2011). Here, the Thai employees in JTHAI are motivated to be family members (the family) who cooperate through seniority (the corporation), helping others (the religion logic) to ultimately gain economic results (the market logic). The benevolence of the Thai leader is strongly implied in the term of family, so its father needs to not only care for the child but also to gain religious merit, not only facilitating but also strengthening both family and religions logics. This practice is consistent with what Greenwood et al. (2010) showed as the relationship between Spanish family-owned firms and Catholicism. It also confirms Bhappu's (2000) identification of family and religion logics within Japanese MNCs. She demonstrates the existence of family and religion logics simply operating within Japanese MNCs, but fails to point out how these logics coexist and cooperate. Logics are likely to intertwine through the meanings of reciprocity. This further elaborates on the concept of amplification, which Greenwood et al. (2011) propose to be the amplified effects of the family and religion logics, because both logics concern social responsibility in society, rather than self-interest.

Moreover, it questions the assumption that Waldorff, Reay, and Goodrick, (2013) made: the facilitative relationship among logic is equal to the amplified relationship for which Greeenwood et al. (2010) argued. Goodrick and Reay (2011) assert that the facilitative relationship gains collective influence to guide practices while the additive relationship guides different expectations without conflicts. In the cases examined here, the amplified relationship can be positioned as a broader concept that involves the facilitative relationship. Furthermore, the Thai employees characterise themselves as 'family' when developing Japanese customers (see 6.3), while also manifesting religious merit in Theravada Buddhism when developing customers (see 6.4). They do not scold or yell as Japanese expatriates do but forgive the mistakes of their subordinates by saying, "*mai pen rai*." Their attributed meanings of religious merit are not only facilitated with, but also amplified by, the demand to generate revenue (the corporation). This indicates amplified relationships among logics that facilitate as well as strengthen themselves.

6.6 Personal reflection: the importance of *ongaeshi* in Japanese society

On reflection, I noticed that the idea of *ongaeshi* legitimises reciprocal interpersonal relationships among Japanese, probably being deeply rooted in Japanese society. A folktale in Japan, called '*Tsuru no Ongaeshi*', directly tells its important value between parents and their children. Once upon a time, a poor young man working on a farm saved a crane injured by a bird hunter. He pulled a sharp arrow from its wing and cleaned the wound so that the bird was able to fly. He luckily returned the bird back to the sky, telling it to 'be careful of bird hunters!'. Then, he moved back home that night and saw a beautiful young woman standing in front of the house. She said to him, 'Welcome home and I'm your wife.' With a big surprise, both started to live together as a couple. Later on, the wife asked the husband to build a weaving room so as to weave cloth for a living but with one condition. She told him, 'Promise me that you would never peek inside.' He promised her, and then, she constantly wove for a week and came out with a beautiful cloth such as he had never seen. It was sold with high price and gave them many coins. They began to become a wealthy couple. One day he wondered how she made such a beautiful cloth, broke the promise, and peeked inside the room. Alas! There was a beautiful crane that was plucking out its feathers and using them as threads. Then, the crane noticed and said, 'I am the crane that you saved before and just wanted to repay you and that's for what I became your wife, but now you have seen my actual form so I can't stay here any longer.' The crane then flew away and disappeared forever.

This folktale indicates the importance of *ongaesh* as legitimised by the *ko-on* relationship mentioned in this chapter. In Japan, once you, as a child, are well treated by your parents, then you need to repay them. Probably the word 'repayment' in English is not exactly synonymous with *ongaeshi* because it strongly implies an economic sense of repaying one's own debts. In an economic sense, the debt is visible and measurable while *on* is not. There is no direct interpretation of this concept into English language. Normally in a Japanese family, the oldest son will be responsible for taking care of his parents after their retirement. This is still a strong social norm, especially in the countryside of Japan and, because of this norm, some friends of mine have decided to stay in their home town, rather than go abroad to experience new and challenge things. One of these friends said to me, 'I cannot leave my parents [in his home town] because I am the oldest.' Like the crane in the folktale, the oldest son, or the oldest daughter if there is no son, is expected to take care of his or her elderly parents. This care is a form of *ongaeshi* ('repayment) for what he or she had received from his or her parents. In my job interview at a university in Osaka, the second-largest city in Japan, I was asked whether I could move there to become a lecturer and said, 'Yes, I can.' Then the interviewer, the dean, asked about my family structure and said, '[B]ut I guess you will need to be back to your home town in the near future to take care of your living parents.' I simply nodded, not denying his comment although I had not thought of it. I clearly realised myself that, in Japan, *oya ko ko, ongaeshi* for parents, is an important part of people's lives. I am sure that *oya ko ko* is one of the phrases which triggers some life changing event for many Japanese, similar to changing a job and/or location, or retirement.

Not only does this concept of *ongaeshi* influence a biological family or even take place within organisations but it even influences a relationship between a buyer and its suppliers. Through my professional experience in a Japanese trading company, this reciprocal relationship continues to be emphasized by seniors and my colleagues. When I was a young salesperson at a Japanese semiconductor trading company, I faced an urgent demand for a price markdown from my customer due to the low price of another vendor. I then passed this request to a contact of the vendor, a large Japanese semiconductor manufacturer, but he, a manager, was deeply sceptical about this request so I brought him to a meeting with the customer. The customer explained that he decided to deal with multiple vendors, eventually leading to a cost markdown. Although the vendor-manager insisted on knowing the exact price, the customer did not take this question and just said, 'Please, ask Iwashita-san later for the details.' This gave me complete discretion as to how much the semiconductor parts needed to be discounted to the vendor, giving me additional margin for my company. This was interpreted as my receiving *on*, a favour, from the customer according to my Japanese manager with whom I shared the event. My manager, on hearing this story, insisted that I bring a gift to the customer in exchange for the favour I received. I was then burdened to repay the customer through business. However, I failed to repay him at this case but expressed appreciation and thanks to him at a next meeting without the vendor. Moreover, even for Japanese people educated abroad, the concept of *ongaeshi* probably still constitutes interpersonal relationships. I still remember that a friend of mine, a Japanese management consultant educated at a business school in the United States, kept telling me the importance of *ongaeshi*: not until the moment he repaid the organisation where he belonged could he have left it. I recently heard that he left his company and initiated his own his business, which made me smile. I am so sure that he must have successfully completed the act of *ongaeshi* to his previous company!

7 Either self-interest or family interest?

Work and employment

7.1 Introduction

This chapter explores how the practices in work and employment are interpreted through competitive relationships between logics. It is organised into three sections. First, job delegation is discussed. Next, performance appraisal is evaluated. Finally, socialisation is reviewed. The concluding section articulates the finding of the chapter: the constellations of logics are ongoing and continuously formed in relation to geographical locations.

7.2 Job delegation: a conflict between self-improvement, self-acceptance and self-interest

Job delegation contextually enacts a conflict among Japanese family, religion, corporation and market logics on an ongoing basis. Theravada Buddhism in JTHAI contextually enacts religious merit gained through self-acceptance, while Japanese family self-improvement is a reciprocal obligation. A conflict arises between Theravada Buddhism and family logics when a Thai director finds it difficult to delegate a job properly. For the Japanese, self-improvement is assumed to be a burden of family members and thus a manager has to help his subordinates to improve. Japanese tend to treat local employees by saying, '*Shita gekirei*', a phrase often used in reference to Japanese family, meaning to give a pep talk while scolding if necessary. In a sense, job delegation is treated as an opportunity for on-the-job training by Japanese managers. In contrast, for Thais, self-acceptance is assumed to be central to gaining religious merit. In fact, a Thai director simply accepts the fact that there may be people incapable of doing the task, completing it by himself instead. This echoes a religious belief that 'one's current status is related to the way one led one's prior lives (Atmiyanandana and Lawler, 2003, p. 235)'. Briefly, Theravada Buddhism enables actors to gain religious merits through acts such as 'kindness towards others, especially the less fortunate (Atmiyanandana and Lawler, 2003, p. 234)'.

Thus, when a Thai director finds it difficult to delegate a job to his subordinates, he sees this as because of a 'prior life' and, therefore, accepts incompetent subordinates as they are by immediately giving up on training and encouraging. A Japanese expatriate exemplifies that:

> There is one [Thai] salesman who is really incapable under a Thai director. So I ordered the Thai director to tell the salesman do a particular job. Then, what happened is that the director did that job instead, not the salesman. Thus the salesman would not be educated nor would he recognise this as an issue because the director did the job instead. I observed that the director already gave up asking the salesman to do the job and did it by himself. He never tried to give a pep talk to the salesman. In brief, he is an individual [not a team member]. [He thinks] he is capable but the other isn't. It means that I am I and you are you. . . . Here, Theravada Buddhism is immensely influential . . .

He explained that this tendency is attributed to the religious aspect of Theravada Buddhism behind the Thai behaviours, the importance of forgiving others mistakes. The Japanese expatriate did not notice this contextual religious aspect in job delegation until the moment when the Thai director did the job instead. The Thai director simply accepts the fact that his staff is incapable while the Japanese tend to feel 'obligated' to encourage their staff until the subordinates become competent. This conflict is triggered by contextual enactment of religion logic, Theravada Buddhism.

On this occasion, the Japanese expatriate would tend to become angry and scold these Thai employees because job delegation enacts Japanese family, which promotes the self-improvement of its members. He interprets this by showing anger as a feature of the father's role to his children in the process of raising them, while it is also a habit of pursuing one's economic contribution. He believes that 'there must be someone who should scold irresponsible salespeople . . . in a sense, I am taking on this burden . . . I am not Thai or will I live here forever . . . this is why I can be mad at local employees who are irresponsible.' It is true that he knows full well how much the Thais dislike being scolded. In a harmony with Thai Theravada Buddhism, it is important to keep face 'in-group' so Thais tend not to show anger or be upset in front of others. Instead, they are smiling and often saying, '*mai pen rai*' ('never mind'). Nonetheless, he would rather adopt the role of a commercial manager to justify the need to care and therefore scold the locals for their irresponsibility. In fact, this Japanese expatriate manager asked my concurrence by saying that:

> The Japanese normally conduct '*Shita Gekirei*' (giving a pep talk while scolding in English) to the young and inexperienced who are incapable of doing something, don't we? The Japanese tend to expect you (as a child) to change in the future, so training you, scolding you when you [are] wrong, advising you, or proposing you with some ideas. . .

This contrasts meanings of job delegation between the Japanese family and Thai Buddhism. The Japanese family prioritises the virtue of self-improvement as a burden of the Japanese family, while Thai Theravada Buddhism sees the virtue of self-acceptance as a religious merit. This Japanese expatriate is convinced that a manager should continuously encourage and supervise his staff regardless of whether or not they are capable, as Kondo (1990) strongly implies. This contrasts with the notion of Theravada, however, which prioritises accepting subordinates as they are and forgiving all the mistakes they make.

In this interview, I completely agreed with him because this echoes my personal working experience at Japanese MNCs. Japanese managers tend to feel obligated to encourage and even to reprimand, if necessary, their subordinates until they become competent. In fact, I was told by supervisors, when at Japanese MNCs, to teach and care for freshmen in the workplace. This type of anger showed by the Japanese expatriate is not interpreted as a negative but rather as a positive behaviour demonstrating care for one's employees. Indeed, the term *shita gekirei* manifests what an ideal family should be: children are to be raised and trained by being given a pep talk and by being scolded whenever necessary.

These constellations of logics can be contextually formed differently in other geographical locations such as in JEU. Here, job delegation is viewed as job efficiency in order to achieve the self-interest of the manager who conducts it. A Belgian operator shares her job delegated by her Belgian manager when she joined JEU. Although she has never worked at Japanese MNCs before, she contrasts the way of working of the Belgian and the current Japanese MD, by stating:

> In the beginning [a Belgian manager] was more controlling. Checking everything; which I can understand because you need to watch a lot of details in the Customer Service Department. He also gave us a bit of room but not so much as [Japanese MD] did. . . . Also depending upon the problem and the personality of the boss, of course, [the manager] wants to protect his own thing and wants to control everything . . .

This comment implies a difference in job delegation between self-improvement and self-interest. The Belgian manager shares how he wants to treat his employees as follows:

> So I really I try to . . . should I say . . . create somebody who can work independently without too much . . . I try to create somebody who can work independently . . . It's more maybe my way, not typically Japanese; I think more my way because I want him to learn things also . . . you can learn by yourself you remember better . . . I give him also targets and within these targets he can manage for himself . . . he has his freedom to work between the targets.

This echoes the job delegation he conducted for her in the past. It manifests the self-interest of the manager in terms of delegating jobs efficiently. He has worked at JEU for a long time, but not had working experience at Japanese MNCs before. The market logic enacted in job delegation constrains actors to efficiently delegate a job to their subordinates so that both can work independently. This indicates that the same practices contextually enact multiple different logics, continuously forming competitive relationships among logics on an ongoing basis. Neither a singular 'victory' or 'defeat' of a particular logic make competitive logics segemented (e.g. Goodrick and Reay, 2011).

7.3 Performance appraisal: bonus, sales incentive and promotion

A bonus and sales incentive can contextually manifest the competitive relationships between Japanese family (family) and self-interest (market) on an ongoing basis. Granted, constellations of logics are contextually enacted, conflicted and contextually mediated on an ongoing basis. However, there is some distinction between Asia and the West. In Asia, a bonus rewards collective performance (i.e. the family logic tends to be manifested) while, in the West, a sales incentive promotes individual performance (the market logic). Nonetheless, constellations of logics are not simply prefixed but contextually enacted on an ongoing basis.

7.3.1 A bonus as a collective reward: Japanese family in the corporation

In Asia, an equally distributed bonus is recognised as a collective reward for collective performance, enacting the Japanese reciprocal family logic. In JTAIW and JTHAI where a bonus is adopted, sales performance is viewed not as an individual performance but as a collective one. This logic conflicts with the market logic, however, with a strong demand for an individual bonus or salary increase from local employees.

Taiwanese salespeople in JTAIW, for example, treat a bonus as a consequence of individual performance. They tend to argue for a greater bonus than that of others who, they think, performed less. For them, a bonus is expected to be distributed according to each salesperson's performance. In particular, in annual salary negotiations, this demand is put forward. A Taiwanese director explains the importance of individual salary:

> . . . I am sales and considering only numbers. The reason why I care about profits and sales is to think about more salary and more incentive to change our life. How can we change life? That can be done by salary, right? Wage, that is salary, right? If we make big numbers, that means that Taiwanese could get more salary. Japanese thinks about the benefit of Tokyo only.

This manifests sales performance as a consequence of individual self-interest (the market logic), not collective (family). Facing a strong demand from his Taiwanese employees, the director favours the importance of individual performance evaluation and a salary increase according to one's performance. A Taiwanese manager echoes the importance of salary by stating: 'I created customers, and achieved big revenue, then I could negotiate an increase in salary with the boss. That is the American style. But in a Japanese company, I am not sure of if they accept it'. This tendency to argue for a salary increase continues especially among Taiwanese local employees. A Taiwanese secretary summarises this demand through her observation as follows:

> There are no Japanese management features here, such as loyalty and harmony . . . an individual Taiwanese salesman appeals his performance to his managers but the bonus amount is almost the same as others. Finally one's bonus is the same as others, usually equal to several months' salary, so they are disappointed. This occurs over and over.

This observation illuminates a confrontation between Japanese family and market logics. There is another Taiwanese director who has worked long at JTAIW. He rather accepts the existence of the family norm by stating, 'But a Japanese company is a family. Competition among employees is less than in an American company. . . . JTAIW is not Taiwanese but Japanese because of its Japanese style.' Then, he states the job security of Japanese companies because Japanese companies do not fire their employees but rather prefer long-term and lifetime employment. For him, a bonus is a collective reward rather than an individual reward. The competitive relationships are continuously formed 'over and over' in everyday practices within JTAIW.

This confrontation between family and market logics, however, is contextually mediated by the corporation logic where an ultimate authority in the corporation tends to be given to the *laopan* (in Chinese 'president'). Actual bonus negotiation are often escalated to the Japanese MD because Taiwanese tend to claim a salary increase directly to the Japanese MD over the heads of Taiwanese managers and directors. In the Taiwanese business, the *laopan* is believed to be the only decision-maker in the corporation. A Japanese expatriate comments that there is a societal effect of the corporation on Taiwanese employees by the *laopan* because, whatever it is, they tend to eventually follow what the *laopan* says and orders. In performance appraisal meetings with the Taiwanese, the Japanese MD asks, 'What do you think really contributes to achieving your sales quota? In other words, is your sales performance achieved solely by your own effort?' He then raises the possibility of other colleagues and experienced managers in helping to coordinate sales opportunities by communicating with the executives in the customer organisations. Finally, the Taiwanese concluded that his sales performance was not solely the result of his own efforts but rather the product of organisational efforts. Salespeople may be reluctantly convinced by this argument but it causes them considerable displeasure. One local Taiwanese salesperson who sought an increase in salary in the past declared: 'I had no choice but to accept his claim . . . he is the president' after his performance appraisal. This manifests ongoing constellations of logics: the corporation logic mediates the market logic in Asia where the authority of the *laopan* through the corporation logic is rooted.

Of course, performance appraisal does not always enact self-interest (the market logic). A Taiwanese director confessed that he could live with his own salary while admitting the fact that the young salespeople tend to put a request for salary increase. He clarifies:

> Comparing with that of my co-workers in the previous workplace, this salary cannot be comparable. It is very poor. As a young salesman's quote, this salary is too low comparing with foreign companies such as even Japanese. . . . But my salary is enough given the fact that I have a house in Taipei city, a wife and a daughter without [a] house mortgage.

According to his situation with his family, the market logic does not enable him to pursue self-interest. Through daily interaction with his subordinates, this is continuously forming a competitive relationship between family and market logics in relation to the corporation logic.

For the Japanese, this competitive relationship between the family and market may look unusual. From the Japanese MD's point of view, this demand is unlikely to happen in Japan because of the importance of *wa* ('organisational harmony'). He went on to say:

> . . . this is a point of difference between the Japanese and Taiwanese . . . the Japanese, in general, will never insist on a salary increase in comparison with others . . . [paused] . . . well, at least, I have never done this in my professional career . . . because it would make me an egotist going against '*Wa*' (organizational harmony in English) from the point of view of others [organisational members].

In the actual interview, after glancing at me, he added the conditional sentence 'at least, I have never done [salary increase]'. At the time, I was bit embarrassed. He added the sentence since I was quiet in respect to his comment of 'the Japanese, in general, will never insist on a salary increase'. From his view, I was not in the category of 'Japanese' because I negotiated with the managers for an increase in my salary in the past when in an American corporation in Japan. His comment raises the importance of *wa* in the Japanese family in performance appraisal regardless of whether one performs better or worse than do others. The market logic based on self-interest sharply contrasts with Japanese family as the corporation.

Likewise, there is a demand for salary increases among non-managerial Thai employees. Some young Thai salespeople often argue for an increase in their individual salary, manifesting self-interest. Unlike the demand in JTAIW for the reward of individual performance, that of JTHAI suffices in exchange for new projects or new business. For instance, in new customer acquisition, Thai local employees often question why they need to expand their business by doing something new. This type of salespeople would tend to leave JTHAI within a few years given the fact that his salary is relatively low compared with other Western companies. A Japanese expatriate describes:

> [Thais'] motivation is . . . money. Given revenue growth every year, [Thais] often ask me why it is bad to keep the status quo . . . [Thais] never understand, although I explained [to] them that, given the fact that market is growing, keeping the current amount of revenue means decreasing market share . . . in initiating some new project, they again ask me how they can be motivated . . . then it boils down to money [sales incentive] . . .

In order to initiate something new, they end up asking for a salary and/or bonus increase as their motivation. A Thai manager illustrates this self-interest by stating: 'no commission can be an issue because it is difficult to motivate sales managers without commissions . . . this may be a common issue at Japanese companies'. The fact that, in the past, one Thai director with a good amount of salary never did anything challenging is consistent with the contextual enactment of the market logic. He was so comfortable with a fixed salary that he did not take proactive actions.

Notwithstanding, this self-interest can be mediated by the enactment of the religion logic. Theravada Buddhism is enacted through an attempt to increase others' salary to solve the emerged competitive relationship between family and market logics. A Thai manager tends to insist on the increase of her subordinates' salary, instead of her own salary. A Japanese expatriate shares this story:

> There was a request that a Thai manager made for an increase in her men's salary while rejecting an increase in her pay, stating that her salary had been raised enough. . . . She reasoned that her men had worked very hard for her . . .

This, albeit superficially looking family sounds like self-sacrifice to do good in a religious context. He went on to connect this event to Theravada Buddhism. Unfortunately, I did not have the chance to interview her. Nonetheless, the manager is believed by the Japanese to have tried to gain religious merit for herself by sharing an increase in her salary with her men. Considering that she devotes herself to work in JTHAI by working late, another Thai manager characterises that 'she must deeply love JapanCo (JTHAI)'. This demonstrates the specific geographical location in Asia where Japanese family is accepted and in turn amplified with the religion norm, such as Theravada Buddhism.

7.3.2 A sales incentive and promotion as an individual reward: self-interest and seniority

The constellations of logics in the West can sharply contrast with those of Asia. In JUSA and JEU, the market logic strongly manifests sales incentives as a means of achieving one's own self-interest based on individual performance. Sales performance in JUSA is individually evaluated without connecting itself to corporate performance. Each customer is assigned to a respective salesperson so there is no space for salespeople to share collective sales goals and to collaborate together. The Japanese VP understands that sales performance appraisals cannot be conducted without the number that reflects the amount of sales commission. So performance evaluation is based only on numbers. He explains:

> It is all about [sales] numbers so I can't help but pay more [salary and sales commission] to the one who performs better [than agreed sales budget] because it will be trouble if he or she leaves [JUSA] . . . I cannot evaluate other than with [numbers] . . .

The strong sense of self-interest is absolute to retain talented salespeople. This is different from JTHAI and JTAIW where performance is measured in a corporate context.

This self-interest has to be achieved through a series of performance appraisals, even for engineers. It means that a high individual evaluation has to directly lead to promotion, a salary increase in other words. A Japanese expatriate supports the view that American individuals are separated from the organisations to which they belong. He commented that 'here [USA], it is common for people to change their jobs for a better salary'. In the past, he conducted a performance appraisal for an American engineer, giving a high evaluation and no change in salary. The engineer was confused and demotivated, and finally left JUSA. He went on to point out the individual aspect of salary separated from the corporate performance:

> Japanese tend to say that you did perform well but our corporate did not. So, sorry to say, but the salary at this time is like this [no change] although I am evaluating you highly . . . Japanese will accept this but [Americans] here will not . . . nor will they be convinced of this . . . [they begin to ask] why don't you raise my salary although my performance was highly evaluated? . . . it leads to rather 'demotivation' . . .

In particular, this 'demotivation' seems to be common in Japanese MNCs in the United States (e.g. Sumihara, 1999). This sharply contrasts with the case in Japan where people tend to stay in the same corporation that they first entered because of the loyalty that they have for the corporation. He simply commented that 'here, people do care about the salary more than Japanese do'. In other words, individual performance is evaluated separately from that of the corporation. Even the salary of a local American salesperson could be twice that of the Japanese VP and American president according to a simple scale of sales incentive.

Unlike the market logic manifesting self-interest in JUSA, promotion in other subsidiaries in Asia and the West is closely associated with seniority (the corporation logic). For example, in JEU, there is a mixture of market and family logics. Here, sales incentives are planned to be replaced by a fixed salary in a current organisational change. The underlying assumption of this change is that 'the salary scale is based on performance and seniority' according to a newly hired HR manager. She went on to imply that although the salary needs to be raised when one performs better, salary and seniority in the corporation are to be balanced: '[B]ut we're not obliged to [raise salary], it's not a company rule or not a Belgium law if somebody is not performing well we can give him not a raise of his salary'. In line with the same assumption, in JTHAI, there were Thai two directors recently promoted: the elder one is a director and the younger an assistant director. A Thai HR manager commented that 'age is not clear criteria . . . we do not have clear criteria seniority, not the length of service'. In fact, there are also 'some elders who work under supervision of the young' according to her. This promotion, however, is apparently the conventional notion of Japanese seniority to reward individual performance.

Likewise, promotion in JTAIW enacts a conventional notion of seniority and length of service (the corporation logic), thereby mediating self-interest (the market logic). A Japanese expatriate director describes, 'Here in [Taiwan] where age is more concerned [than other] so the organisation where the young supervises the old does not really fit in'. So he tends to hire and assign the positions of managers and non-managerial employees in alignment with seniority. He confessed to the importance of seniority:

> [People] have different jobs, different abilities, different ages, and different family structures, so I am sceptical if only numbers can be criteria [in performance appraisal] . . . I am by no means saying or intending to mean that Japanese seniority is good yet neither performance based salary nor sales incentive is compatible with our business . . .

His business is in building equipment that needs teamwork and a long-term relationship with customers. A Japanese MD has a slightly different view of seniority, which may be outweighed by the length of service according to payment claims from Taiwanese employees. He has heard of requests for salary increases based on the length of service, not seniority. He shared a conversation with a Taiwanese manager regarding the performance appraisal of its salesperson. He stated that 'well, this man is already 32 years old and has kids so said why don't you raise his salary . . . but [the Taiwanese manager] told me it's irrelevant'. For the Taiwanese, the corporation logic is implicated only in the length of service but for the Japanese it is implicated in seniority alongside Japanese family. This indicates that self-interest (the market logic) enacted by promotion is mediated by seniority and or the length of service (the corporation logic).

7.4 Socialisation: intensive and minimum socialisations

Social occasions can enact competitive relationships between Japanese family and market logics on an ongoing basis. There are meaningful distinctions between Asia and West. In Asian subsidiaries, such as JTHAI and JTAIW, family logic enables actors to have frequent formal and informal social occasions, forming a family norm among members. In contrast, in the West, such as JEU and JUSA, there are few social events, which enable actors to treat themselves as independent professionals. Here, family norm is little identified and even negated by the actors. The geographical locations do not entirely determine the competitive relationships, however. There are competitive relationships between logics enacted by the actors in their contexts.

7.4.1 Intensive socialisation as an opportunity for family and religious merits

In Asia, regular corporate events manifest reciprocal family logic. In JTHAI and JTAIW, there are company parties and company trips. Either a yearly company party or a company trip is sponsored and conducted by both subsidiaries. In particular, in JTHAI, there are further events such as dinners and lunches, even gym workouts together. At the company parties, there are pieces of music, dance and games played by the Thai employees. Some even brought specific costumes. A Japanese expatriate mentioned that 'they all seem to enjoy the socials . . . some well prepared for pieces of dances, songs, and comedies . . . these [many socials] are quite common in Thailand'. There is even a department trip that is volunteered for by department members without corporate support. In line with these socials, Thai employees characterise themselves as family. Japanese family is strongly manifested in frequent formal and informal social occasions.

For the Japanese, these practices are all welcomed, being consistent with the family logic operating in the JapanCo group. However, for the Thais, these events can be the moments when they not only build a father-and-child relationship between a manager and his subordinates but also gain religious merits for themselves. These can also be occasions when they gain religious merits by letting the Japanese pay for all dinners or lunches. For instance, a Japanese expatriate from the engineering department often goes out for meals with Thai employees. He shows his frustration by saying:

> . . . I often went out for lunch and dinner with my subordinates (Thai employees) . . . I have always paid for meals for the last few years but I have never ever been thanked by them . . . NEVER! . . . well, I do not mean to stop going out with them but sometimes I am strongly discouraged by this . . .

This enacts the Theravada Buddhism merit of *tam bun* in Thai, while superficially looking like a typical practice of Japanese management enacting family logic. One of the reasons behind the apparently unthankful attitude of the Thais is closely associated with gaining religious merits on the basis that the 'haves' help the 'have-nots'. From the Thais' view, the Japanese behaviour of treating them to meals look like that of gaining a religious merit, helping others, and they therefore respond by not offering thanks. Agreeing with this religious behaviour that the researcher had pointed out in the interview, another Japanese manager argued that some Thais showed a thankful attitude to him after paying for their dinner. He says:

> [Because of Buddhism, no thanks from a Thai] is quite normal but that also depends on his personality. My engineers sometime say "Thank you" to me when I take them out for lunch.

He normally pays for all the lunches and dinners with the Thai employees. He explains that when Thais go out for lunch or dinner, the richest in the group has to pay for all the meals. A Japanese expatriate describes this in Thailand as 'a religious culture where one who has more money than the others should pay all'. However, another Japanese expatriate shares some exceptional experience when going out for lunch with Thais. He describes:

> One time, when I dined out for lunch with one Thai who had just been promoted, I was told that 'You do not need to take a bill today because I am promoted so I will pay for this, Thank you'. So it depends on one's moral position and etiquette. It further depends on if one can greet me when entering and leaving the office.

This conflicting interpretation demonstrates that the practices superficially manifest as family but the religion logic, especially the importance of gaining religious merits in Theravada Buddhism, supports the contention that it is actors who make competitive relationships between logics (Smets and Jarzabkowski, 2013). In this case, this religion logic may operate with the family in a distinctive manner. Even in social events, a small distinction between family and religion often suffices.

This intensive socialisation enacting family and religion is questioned by the Japanese MD in JTHAI who asks if this is economically efficient. It often involves not only local employees but also several contacts of Japanese customers, thus incurring a hefty bill. The current Japanese MD claims that:

> [Dinners] with the customers are fine. But what are these for? If it were for information exchange, [a Thai manager] should not have called a gorgeous dinner, inviting 7–8 persons from the customers and 3–4 persons from us, spending a large amount of money on it. . . . What is the purpose of it? It was just for eat and drink. He was just asked a dinner by a customer. . . . Hey, you as a manager, think! He, as a leader, needs to see always balance [between its purpose and actions].

This comment shows the president's concern about economic efficiency in socialisation. By contrast, the local Thai managers simply organise dinners for benevolence to the Japanese customers while the Japanese president evaluates the efficiency return on investment by having dinners. These different interpretations in socialisation are a vivid example of competitive relationships between the family, religion and market logics.

Japanese family logic enacted by intensive socialisation can be connected to the actors' daily work. There is an instrumental aspect of Japanese family logic for economic efficiency. Certainly, a Thai director purposefully builds and uses the concept of family to get his subordinates to take on work for which they are not formally responsible. In order to deal with an overwhelming number of sales inquiries, he tries to share sales jobs with other sales support teams who are not responsible for these inquiries. In a sense, he finds an opportunity to utilise this notion of family for his own economic benefit and strategically uses the concept of family to execute job efficiency. He states:

> If some claim that this is not my job, then I have nothing to say. But a family relationship helps others to collaborate beyond their job descriptions. The job description is just a paper to know basic responsibilities. Then, the family could help with others.

For him, maintaining a family-like relationship is a means to achieve the aim of sharing jobs efficiently and effectively for Japanese customers. He purposefully creates and intentionally uses the family atmosphere to assign a job flexibly by communicating in a friendly manner with his subordinates. He went on to explain, 'In order to set up intimate family relationship, I use informal and casual languages to my subordinates as to my brothers and sisters. For others outside of the division, I use more formal language. With this family-like relationship, my subordinates casually come to consult me.' In fact, by perceiving his communication style, some corporate staff describe his team in building automation as very much a 'Japanese one', which seems to directly belong to JHQ, not to JTHAI. This instrumental aspect of the family relationship is reinforced through the language that is used in everyday practice.

7.4.2 *Minimum socialisation as opportunity for maintaining independent professionals*

In the other subsidiaries, the Japanese family norm, as previously reviewed, is rarely identified and even strongly denied by actors through few socials events. Instead, independent economic professional relationships are implicated in social events in the remaining subsidiaries. In particular, in JUSA, there are few social events. A few social events enact the norm of self-interest to keep professional relationships among employees to a bare minimum. A female sales support describes its norm as 'very professional', which echoes the comment by an American director who characterise JUSA as an 'American company'. She then adds, '[other employees] and myself actually go across the street at lunch hour and work out together so we try to keep it social as well so we're not always trying to kill each other'. After being asked if there is family norm in social events, she is dead against the existence of family as at JTHAI and claims that:

> No it's not like a family here. I will put my 40 hours in. I will work my 8–5 and I will do everything I can to my best while I'm here, 5 o'clock I'm out that door, bye bye. Don't call me. I don't stay. I come in early maybe 15, 20 minutes but I can get a lot done while the phones are not ringing and if I don't get everything done I will stay later to make sure everything is accomplished for that day, but I don't feel like it's a family at all no . . . I would say it's quite professional.

Here, the market logic, commoditising work time as price, is strongly manifested among local employees and in social events. This concept of investment and return echoes other American employees who characterise social events as 'professional' for smooth interpersonal relationships, not for creating or maintain family relationships.

Notwithstanding, there is another view that promotes social events, indirectly implicating the Japanese family. By admitting the fact of a few socials, an American VP expresses his feeling about socialisation in JUSA in comparison with that of the Japanese MNC at which he used to work. He describes:

> Not enough, in my opinion . . . Not like in Japan. For example, when I go to [another office] California, you know, I always just ask and I will always go out, you now, lunch or some dinner or something, some place, because that is quite common for us and we will have some discussion, but me and my President, never.

Then, he confesses that the American president always declines his invitation for meals so he never had a chance to go out with the president. Indeed, there are no company trips or dinners except for a Christmas party. Nor is there a company polo shirt as at JTHAI.

Similarly, in JEU, there are now more social events that tend to enact economic efficiency (the market logic) through professional relationships. In the past, layoffs occurred and the corporate norm here is not collaborative. Members do not trust each other, especially the former Japanese MD. He was treated as 'an enemy' by locals because he conducted restructuring in a bad way. In previous social events, none of locals wanted to be seated next to him. Now there is a new Japanese MD and company meetings are conducted in a friendly atmosphere once again, according to the interviews. A Belgium salesperson states:

> We have every two months, we have our company meeting and then it's two days and then on . . . then of course we have lunch together and then one evening we always go out to have dinner together.

A Belgium director also explains the recent transition from the previous to the current Japanese MD:

> I think the social events are much more because with Mr [the previous Japanese president] there were nearly no social events so I think Mr [the current Japanese president] is getting more like social events but I think that building a team or doing some team building activities are really necessary for the company because it is still not a fully complete team. It's still quite isolated. It's much better than two years ago but I think there's still a lot to do.

So these social events are now used to build JEU as a team. In line with JUSA, interpersonal relationships in social events are professional. These comments sharply contrast with those in the previous subsection, which demonstrates Japanese family mediated by the Thai religion, Theravada Buddhism.

Likewise, the professional relationship is emphasised in terms of the market logic in JTAIW. Although there are company social events like party and trips, Taiwanese tend to limit socialisation to a bare minimum. For instance, despite formal social events, company trips and parties, there seem to be few informal social events. A Taiwanese manager states:

> Social events such as dinners and lunch are not frequent: once in two or three months. Other members know my family but I do not know others through company trips. There are not many chances.

Many of the local employees characterise the relationship among them as predominantly professional with few informal social events. A female administrator supports the few socials by saying that 'it is professional . . . we go out for dinner about once a year . . . I go out as my department group but not informally [for developing my private relationship]'. This may relate to Chinese family logic that locates their group of family stakeholders outside the corporation. Their social group does not overlap with the members of the corporation. This indicates ongoing constellations of logics that are reinforced in everyday practices.

7.5 Discussions and conclusions

The purpose of this chapter was to understand how the practices in work and employment are interpreted through the competitive relationships between logics. There is a finding identified in this chapter: the constellations of logics are ongoing and continuously formed in relation to geographical locations. This is because, in practice, contextually enacted logics do not necessarily 'win' or 'lose' for lengthy periods of time. Although there are means to deal with and finally resolve the competitive relationships: 'actors' active 'collaboration' (Reay and Hinnings, 2005; 2009) or 'compartmentalisation' (Greenwood et al., 2011) these are not adopted here to mediate the competitive relationship. Rather, negotiation and conflict continue to be played out by actors on an ongoing basis. Both bonus and sales incentives enact multiple logics, continuously forming constellations of logics. In promotion, self-interest (the market), for instance, is emphasised by the Taiwanese while mediated by the corporation logic in Taiwanese *laopan* (see 7.3.2). As another instance, Japanese family enacted by Thais asserting that 'we are family', conflicts with Theravada Buddhism at bill payment (see 7.4.1). In addition, it conflicts with the market efficiency expected by Japanese managing directors. This stems from the notion that constellations of logics are parts of a dynamic and ongoing process of enacting logics. This fact questions the simple notion of 'winner' or 'loser' logics (Thornton, 2004) and blended logics (Thornton et al., 2012), blending elements from different logics, 'organisational filter' and 'field level structure' and possibly determining actors' actions (Greenwood et al., 2011).

This further negates the concept of one-off 'segmenting', which aims to separate the impacts of logics on different actors, geographical communities and organisations once and for all to solve the conflicts caused by competitive relationships (Goodrick and Reay, 2011). Here, actors are situated in their contexts so some see opportunities while others see constraints within the same practices on an ongoing basis. In job delegation, Thai employees, for instance, tend to find opportunities to engage with the religion logic when pursuing sales opportunities with Japanese expatriates. These negate the simple articulation of institutional complexity as an effect of the organisational fields, a group of organisations of JapanCo in this case. Rather, actors act differently according to their background and their contexts. Furthermore, this reveals a serious limitation in the feasibility of the 'organisational filter' proposed by Greenwood et al. (2011). This sheds light on the situatedness of actors, which has only rarely been articulated in the current literature (e.g. Delbridge and Edwards, 2013; Smets and Jarzabkowski, 2013). Therefore, constellations of logics are not automatically formed as a result of societal effects or 'organisational filters' but are created by actors in contexts (Delbridge and Edwards, 2007; 2013). The notion of organisational filter and attributes may lead to reifying organisations as abstract entities, thereby neglecting the dynamic processes building complexity that are demonstrated in this chapter.

Moreover, the constellations of logics are, to some extent, different in Asia and the West. This elaborates the geographical communities in which specific logics are rooted (Lounsbury, 2007; Marquis and Lounsbury, 2007). In Asia, the 'family' logic is enacted through the practices of employment. In JTHAI and JTAIW, actors tend to treat bonuses as a collective reward (see 7.3.1), prioritising group performance over individual performance. In particular, a Thai manager insists on an increase in salary for her men by stating that her salary is raised enough, enacting the religious merit of Theravada Buddhism. Social events are active and there are even company trips and parties (see 7.4.1). This echoes the work of Abo (2015) who argues for geographical locations that may influence Japanese management practices. By contrast, in the West, market logic is strongly enacted by performance appraisal and socialisation (see 7.3.2). Sales incentives and promotion are interpreted as individual rewards while no bonus is adopted. There are few social events (see 7.4.2), thus professionals' relationships are kept to a bare minimum, rather than building a family norm as in JTHAI. As Abo (2015) and Lounsbury (2007) point out, the geographical location matters.

This does not mean that the geographical locations in Asia and the West automatically determine the competitive relationships between logics, however. In JTAIW, despite company trips and parties, there seem to be few informal social events: Taiwanese tend not to go out together as in JTHAI. In JTHAI, some Thai employees make an effort to argue for salary increases when assigned a job in sales development, acquiring new customers or projects. Furthermore, the American director, who had worked at large Japanese automotive manufacturers, insists that JUSA is 'an American company now, but however is going to be Japanese company'. Thus, actors in their contexts are deeply associated with the enactment of competitive logics, but the geographical locations do not determine the relationships between them as the situatedness of actors is discussed (e.g. Delbridge and Edwards, 2013; Smets and Jarzabkowski, 2013). These practices can be due to 'both intentional and unintentional outcomes' in the 'everyday getting by of individuals' (Lawrence et al., 2011). After all, constellations of logics and institutional complexity need to be treated as a dynamic and ongoing process of enacting institutional logics as another constellation of logics.

7.6 Personal reflection: the uneasy relationship between salary and family loyalty

In Japanese MNCs, the relationship between salary and family loyalty is uneasy. This relationship is always a trade-off: one, normally family loyalty is prioritised over another, or individual salary. In my research, I found many Japanese corporations, not only JapanCo but also other Japanese manufacturers in Asia, tend to pay the amount of salary for their local employees in between that of Western and local corporations in the Asian region. I asked them the reason it is in between the Western and local corporations to the effect that heard consistent answers and to want to appeal to family loyalty over the amount of individual salaries in exchange for job stability and security. Some local employees shared their opinions about the uneasy relationship between salaries and family loyalty. Some Japanese say that the locals wanting a large amount of salary will not fit in with the company. Teamwork and collectivism are based on many elements of management, salary, performance and organising and coordinating work and social events. For many Japanese expatriates, a high salary is strongly associated with the employees who are selfish and keen to be greedy. In fact, those who stick to the amount of salary and insist on an increase in their salary, as described in this chapter, are not welcomed and are disgraced by Japanese expatriates.

Likewise, in my research, there was a similar case in a subsidiary of the Toyota group in the United States. There was a very competent and cooperative American female executive in their plant. She was expected to be appointed as a member of the executive board in the near future as the first American board member whom their management team longed for to fulfill the policy of management localisation. She understood well enough the importance of teamwork and sharing information to maintain the quality of their products and services. At the point when their management decided to promote her into the leadership position, she showed up in the office of one executive and told him that she wanted to resign from the company. She was headhunted by an American manufacturer with an almost three times higher salary than that she was receiving. The Japanese executive first tried to get her to stay at the company but soon gave up after her offer of a tripled amount of salary, and eventually accepted her request of resignation. When I interviewed him, he disclosed his feelings by saying that 'it is almost impossible to persuade her to stay'. He could increase her salary in a given range where the salaries of other current elder executives are higher than hers. If he then admitted to tripling the amount of her salary in the Japanese subsidiary, this would have destroyed *wa*, the organisational harmony where the salaries of all the executives are ordered by seniority. The tripled amount of salary would have been higher than that of the CEO of their headquarters in Japan where there is already an invisible glass ceiling of the salaries of not only non-Japanese but also Japanese employees.

Rarely does this apply to Western, especially American, MNCs given their case in Japan. A while ago, at IBM Japan where I used to work as marketing manager, the person who received the highest salary was not the country president but a system engineer (SE). Their country president means the top of IBM Japan. SEs play an important role of delivering a highest value to their customers, and therefore, are supposed to be highly paid, even higher than that of the top. Furthermore, at another American IT company in Japan, a young Japanese manager, based on his performance to his president for a promotion. Rather than wait for his direct boss, a director, to do this on his behalf, he made this contact directly, and eventually got the promotion. The background to this situation is that the manager did not think his performance was properly evaluated by his director, so he was frustrated and finally made overhead diplomacy. I found that, for Japanese MNCs, a trade-off relationship between salary and family loyalty is strongly assumed albeit not manifested all the time in the workplace. It is about a choice between the two.

8 Profiles of Japanised managers

Work organisation

8.1 Introduction

This chapter discusses how the practices in work organisations communicating with JHQ are interpreted through ceremonial aspects and how actors in turn are organised. It also corresponds primarily, but not exclusively, to the third research question of how Japanese and locals are organised, in addition to the cultural meanings of practices (see 2.3). It is organised into three sections. First, communication about expatriate evaluation is reviewed. Second, communication about business results is demonstrated. Third, communication about locals' complaints is presented. In a summarising section, the boundaries of organisational communities are not segmented to Japanese expatriates but constructed through actors' profiles.

8.2 Communicating expatriate evaluation: separated organisational communities of Japanese expatriates

Communication about expatriate evaluation manifests the corporation logic in terms of the organisational hierarchy of Japanese expatriates in their separation from local employees. The performance of Japanese expatriates is evaluated based on JHQ's view, not the subsidiaries' view. Furthermore, in the subsidiaries, the performance of Japanese expatriate managers, regardless of whether they are formally under a local director or president in their site, is set and evaluated by a top-ranked Japanese expatriate in each subsidiary.

Their formal organisational charts simply show who does what in each organisation, but not who manages and assesses what. This causes 'two management structures' (Elger and Smith, 2005) in the subsidiaries. Two structures also allow the family norm to be bounded to Japanese organisational communities.

This ceremonial aspect emerges from tension between the organisational hierarchy (the corporation logic) and an in-group of family ('family logic). For Japanese expatriate managers, their real bosses are not local director employees, albeit some are supposed to report to local directors in their formal organisational

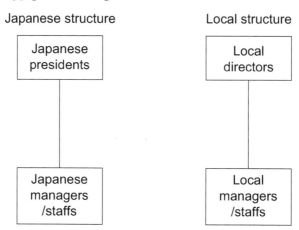

Figure 8.1 The organisational structures for Japanese and locals

charts. All of the Japanese expatriate managers are controlled and managed by a top-ranked Japanese expatriate in their site, regardless of whether they are directly underneath him. A Japanese VP in JUSA claims that there is complete separation between Japanese and locals by saying, '[T]here are five Japanese expatriates including me in the US . . . I am the only one who evaluates the performance of them . . . the American president does not.' The titles of the other Japanese expatriates whom he has to manage range from managers to non-managerial expatriates. In brief, the formal organisational charts do not exactly reflect the positions of Japanese expatriates, and therefore can be seen as ceremonial. This elaborates the divide between Japanese and locals as an export of the two-tier system in Japan, of core and peripheral employees (*seishain* and non-*seishain* in Japanese) (Kopp, 1999).

This separation between Japanese and locals is closely associated with the term 'localisation', which is firmly believed by Japanese expatriates to be an economically efficient institutionalised rule. That is, each business in the overseas market should be developed and managed by local employees. There is no policy that explicitly articulates localisation. Neither is it measured nor evaluated by JHQ or its subsidiaries as the formal organisational goal. Nonetheless, many Japanese expatriates take localisation for granted as the ideal picture in each subsidiary. Granted, a Japanese director in JTAIW picks up the comment which he has received from JHQ, saying, 'What Japan [JHQ] is always saying is that Japanese jobs [by Japanese customers locally] will not last forever so it will be hopeless unless we expand the businesses to local customers in the future.' Thus, he has been pressed by JHQ to develop local non-Japanese customers and localise the management team to support the local customers in the future. Indeed, a Japanese MD in JTAIW, conforming to the institutionalised rule of localisation, asserts that his primary role is 'to identify and train a next local leader', although nobody at JHQ articulates this role explicitly. This pressure from JHQ, however, enables localisation to be institutionalised and eventually to function as a ration-alised myth (Meyer and Rowan, 1977).

Furthermore, there is a structural divide between Japanese expatriates' perfor-mance and their subsidiaries' performance. Japanese expatriates' salary and bonus are evaluated in line with the JapanCo group's performance separate from their subsidiaries' performance. Furthermore, a Japanese expatriate, the president of JTAIW, adds that his performance and bonus are not linked to the performance in Taiwan. He confesses:

> Unfortunately, my salary is not connected to business performance here . . . I submit my performance assessment sheet to the headquarters including the total performance of this subsidiary . . . but the assessment of the bonus, the amount of the bonus is based on the performance of JapanCo as a whole, according to the consolidated financial performance of JapanCo group . . . it is not related to the performance of JTAIW . . .

The salary of Japanese expatriates is basically being provided from the pocket of JHQ, not that of the subsidiary. He sees this as a problem, potentially making Japanese expatriates not responsible for local performance. His bonus would go up when JapanCo group's performance is good, and go down when it is bad. In this process of assessment, they are supposed to be evaluated by the top-ranked Japanese expatriate in each site despite their titles and positions. Because of this evaluation system, Japanese expatriates are expected to work for, not local busi-ness, but the top Japanese expatriate in each site. The line of assessment is invis-ible yet recognised by local employees. A local employee tends to say that '[a Japanese expatriate] is different from local . . . he is from Japan'. Assessments by the top Japanese expatriate in each site go back to the companies, the divi-sions who are responsible for these expatriate managers. This strongly echoes the centralised decision making in Japanese MNCs pointed out by Westney (1987; 1999).

The way of assessing the performance of Japanese expatriates derives from the company's strong focus on the domestic market in Japan. JapanCo group has only 10 per cent of total revenue from the overseas market, being in the initial stage of internationalisation. In actual expatriate evaluation, Japanese expatriates are likely to be aligned with and compared to other Japanese managers working in Japan, despite that the business environments between Japan and overseas are fundamentally different. That is, Japanese expatriates cannot be promoted based on their performance but only relative to other managers' performance in Japan. This may give a disadvantage to Japanese expatriate managers by limiting their opportunities for promotion. A Japanese director in Taiwan illustrates how difficult Japanese expatriates can find it to be promoted as a manager while in overseas subsidiaries, commenting:

> For example, a subsidiary wants me to be promoted as a manager, and gives me a good mark . . . at the headquarters, the company in Japan gets candidate

managers lined up in front and then may say, this man is not really as good as others so he needs to wait [to become a manager] . . . in this sense, the division decides when I can become a manager . . . it has a full authority in respect to personnel affairs across Japan and overseas, and even of where it can allocate and assign managers . . .

This central authority in JHQ creates a divide between Japanese expatriates and local employees. Most Japanese expatriate managers who are dispatched from the division of the in-house company in JHQ are entitled to be promoted in line with other managers by the division in Japan. Furthermore, Japanese expatriates are temporary managers who are supposed to be transferred to somewhere else normally every few years, or five to six years at a maximum. This strong focus on the authority of JHQ highlights the dominant yet separated positions of Japanese expatriates (Kopp, 1999). The domestic market oriented view underlies the expatriate evaluation system and in turn there are two management structures for Japanese and local communities.

In addition to the performance evaluation of Japanese expatriates separate from that of their subsidiaries, their perceived limitations in understanding local culture and customs parallel two management structures. One of the largest barriers that many Japanese expatriates agree about is language. Across all the four subsidiaries, local languages are very different from Japanese, the first language of all the Japanese expatriates. The Japanese VP in JUSA claims that Japanese could not understand Americans thoroughly because of cultural and linguistic differences. He comments that 'having said cultural differences, I think that we Japanese have difficulties understanding everything Americans think'. He firmly believes that the languages, cultures and conditions where Japanese and American are born and raised are fundamentally different and the gaps between them, therefore, cannot easily be filled.

Actors' interpretations go along with Japanese communities in two management structures. A Japanese expatriate in JTHAI is also aware of these two structures and intentionally keeps a distance from local employees, drawing the boundary of family with only Japanese. As a leader developing Japanese customers in Thailand, he continues to locate himself as a role model for local employees by separating himself from the locals. He implies two distinctive groups of actors, Japanese and locals, by commenting:

> Personally, I try not to get along with local employees too much . . . I do not mind that Japanese get along together . . . because I want to form the impression that Japanese do work hard. . . . I am also close to management positions . . . if I am so friendly with locals, others might see me, I think, as no good . . .

The sense of becoming a role model for local employees remains stronger in Thailand where many Japanese customers demand a leadership role for Japanese expatriates. Japanese expatriates become organisational communities spanning boundaries between their subsidiaries, JHQ, and, if any, Japanese customers.

Indeed, Japanese expatriates are considered as separated organisational communities from their subsidiaries by local employees. A Taiwanese secretary at JTAIW made a remark implying the cultural hierarchy behind communications with JHQ. She states:

> I have been to JHQ several times. At JHQ, Japanese seem to believe only Japanese. In exchanging emails, although I am the contact person, JHQ rather comes in contact with my [Japanese] director via email. It passes through me.

Communicating with only Japanese between JHQ and their subsidiaries reinforces two management structures. The trusted relationship among only Japanese echoes Japanese organisational communities reinforced by their particular HR system, benefits and cultural understanding of Japan. Furthermore, the comment of the American president echoes these trusted relationships between Japanese. He states:

> Having seen reports [of JapanCo group]. . . that I have seen within JapanCo, at this point still, is that local staff were, I've even seen it reported on some forms, they call employees at the subsidiaries local stuff. I'm sure they meant local staff and the translation was wrong, but I've seen things where JapanCo employees were almost not considered part of the JapanCo group. . . . It just gives the impression that either we're not trusted or it's kind of difficult to explain.

This articulation of 'stuff', albeit miswritten, manifests mental separation between Japanese and locals. He did not forget to remind me of correct phrases of local stuff: 'I think it should be JapanCo Group Employee.' This strongly implies not only structural but also mental separation between Japanese expatriates and local employees.

This separation between Japanese and locals is consistent across all the subsidiaries. On reflection, it is true that I, as a researcher, go out for lunches and dinners while in the various sites but never had these with local employees. It seems that Japanese expatriates get along with only Japanese and are separated from local employees. In a sense, the family norm does not prevail in the same manner for Japanese and locals. This supports the comment of Kopp (1999), who asserts that this divide sounds like the exportation of the two-tier HRM system in Japan between *seishain* and non-*seishain*, core and peripheral Japanese employees. In Japan, core employees are in permanent contract and thus receive long-term benefits, such as lifetime and long-term employment, seniority-based compensation, and high investment in training, while peripheral employees are on temporary contract and thus gain few benefits. Likewise, this situation is replicated between Japanese expatriates and local employees: Japanese are *seishain* while local employees are non-*seishain*. My initial hunch on this division was confirmed in the next two sections.

8.3 Communicating business results: contested boundaries of organisational communities

Communication about business results manifests actors' interpretations of the corporation logic, making work organisation ceremonial. Localisation as the institutionalised rule is well adopted in JUSA in terms of an American being appointed as the president. It becomes a rationalised myth, however, in the sense that the contact person in charge with communicating with JHQ is not the American president but the Japanese VP. The Japanese VP made a remark on the odd roles and responsibilities between him and the American president, insisting that he needs to be responsible for reporting to JHQ:

> The reasons why a local president is assigned [JUSA] is to build and sustain local business adapting it to local regulations . . . so there is a local president, but from the views of the headquarters I become the president who is accountable for all the businesses here . . . so this has nothing to do with formal organizational chart . . . who is responsible for reporting local businesses to the headquarters is me . . .

It sounds as if the American president is superficially in charge and, nonetheless, the Japanese VP is essentially in charge of managing the local business in the United States. Localisation here functions as a rationalised myth that locals need to be top managers even if they are not capable of communicating in Japanese well.

The actors' linguistic skills of communicating in Japanese are required in communication with JHQ. For example, the Japanese VP, albeit not the top, has far better access to, connection to and knowledge of JHQ than the American president does. The Japanese VP discloses the form of communication with the headquarters:

> There is much information from Japan which does not actually come to [the American president] . . . in a nutshell it is all Japanese [language] . . . personnel affairs, requests to write management reports, customer information, strategic information from sales and marketing departments, and newly appointed executives and directors in Japan . . . this information will not reach him unless I translate it into English . . . it will not be communicated to him [until it is translated] . . .

In practice, the American president owns the managerial information far less than the Japanese VP does, because all the incoming information from Japan is usually articulated in Japanese, which makes the American president powerless and merely a ceremonial president. This highlights ethnocentric features, as Westney points out (1987; 1999), in which Japanese expatriates tend to be dominant in decision making in their subsidiaries. The Japanese VP actively gets the American president involved in this variety of information from Japan by translating it into English to facilitate 'active participation' (Kondo, 1990) from the American president.

Although 'the American president is incapable', as they say, of doing management jobs except for finance, both Japanese and American actors often share the collective responsibility as a feature of family members, thus maintaining this ceremonial organisational structure (corporation). There are three interpretations of the position of Japanese expatriates, as shown in Figure 8.2.

Interpretation number one is based on the formal organisational structure: the Japanese VP underneath the American president. Interpretation number two reflects the JHQ's perspective: the point of contact at JUSA is the Japanese VP, not the American president. Indeed, the American president constantly needs help from the Japanese VP in order to communicate with JHQ. Interpretation number three recognises that the Japanese and American leaders have to collaborate together. The Japanese and American act as a pair in communicating with JHQ, although the Japanese VP has more access to JHQ. This is not economically efficient, but it is, at least, consistent with the current organisational hierarchy. Both actors are considered to share the same responsibility.

A good illustration of interpretation number three is the country managers' meeting at JHQ in Tokyo, Japan. All of the country managers and all of the presidents get together quarterly at JHQ to formally report on their business. In the case of JUSA, a pair of American and Japanese leaders attends this quarterly presentation. The Japanese VP lets the American president present in the meeting the materials which he created. In a sense, in communicating with headquarters, the American president turns into a ceremonial person who makes the formal presentation only but does not know its contents. The fact that the American president

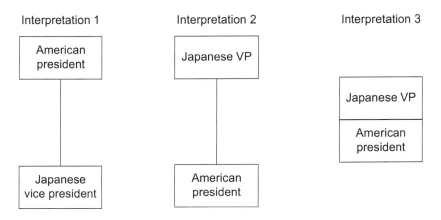

Figure 8.2 Three interpretations of the positions of the Japanese expatriate

cannot speak Japanese or understand what the business is about enforces his position as ceremonial. In the formal organisational chart, it is obvious that the American president is at the top and the Japanese VP is located directly underneath the president (see Figure 5.14).

The ceremonial aspects constructed by localisation as a rationalised myth are also due to the actors' interpretation of a hierarchy (corporation) in their minds between Japan and the West. While admitting that the position of the American president is ceremonial at JUSA, the Japanese VP emphasised that this structure has considerable benefits in terms of its functionality and impression. This supports the culturally interpreted hierarchy in his mind between the Americans and the Japanese, meaning that the American is superior to the Japanese.

> In America . . . given the categories West and Asia, the Japanese are underneath the Americans [the United States] . . . for sure, we are underneath so it would cause conflicts when Japanese try to take a leadership role, however, it would go well when an American is assigned as a leader . . . This does not mean I let him do whatever he wants. Therefore, I always need to remind him about JapanCo's business and how to coordinate with others and to report to JHQ. . . . [Behind the American] I still need to coordinate with surrounding activities in order to receive all the necessary information.

This indicates the Japanese cultural interpretation of Americans, which have historically been established by the relationships between the United States and Japan. Here, he utilises the idea of American leadership in the formal organisational chart but, in practice, he plays a central role in coordinating resources and communicating with JHQ. In line with this cultural interpretation, as well as functional necessity, both actors actively share collective responsibility and in turn collaborate with each other and maintain this ceremonial structure.

This ceremonial aspect may be deeply associated with the notion of the West in Japanese minds. For Japanese expatriates, the Western regions, including Europe, are more respected than in Japan, possibly generating a different response to the local employees. A Japanese expatriate MD who used to work in Asia and Europe shares his impression about the cultural hierarchy between Japan, Asia, and the West. Reflecting on his appointment of a director at JEU, he comments that:

> I did not think that Europeans have ears to listen to a stranger coming from Asia. It was surprising to hear that some Europeans seem to believe that Europe is the centre of the world! [Laugh] Indeed, they do have rich history, industrial civilisation, intellectual culture, and pride . . . they are superior to us, indeed. It would be good to facilitate business environments and motivate them to work as a team rather than to command and control them.

During his tenancy, he tends to delegate his authority as much as possible to European employees. This strongly echoes the current Japanese MD in JEU who comments that 'Europe has historically been above us [Japan]'. This also echoes the comment of the Japanese VP in JUSA saying that 'given the categories West and Asia, the Japanese are underneath the Americans'.

In practice, the ceremonial aspects are mediated by the Japanese family logic, which enables actors to share the same responsibilities. The current Japanese VP clarifies that both he and the American president share the same responsibilities in the profits and losses of the business by saying that:

> [our] responsibilities, a very difficult term to explain . . . it is obvious that a president is accountable for its businesses . . . the American president, of course, needs to report the business performance to Japan on a formal report line . . . but when it comes to the contents of the businesses . . . when you look at the numbers, the numbers are just numbers and will not tell more than the numbers . . . I [as the VP] writes its contents [behind the numbers] . . . which types of customers were approached and what types of businesses were acquired, why these projected numbers turned into actual figures . . .

This indicates they are sharing the same responsibilities to sustain and eventually mediate the ceremonial aspect. This structure does not only rest on a linguistic problem that the American president could not understand Japanese but also depends on his limited knowledge and experience of business. As a result, the collective responsibility and authority are shared by the American and the Japanese. In fact, the Japanese VP has extensive experience at JapanCo group: he began his career with JapanCo in Japan and has a well-developed network within the JapanCo group due to his 20-year career. This network manifests in the extended boundaries of family members on the assumption that the American president actively participates in family matters.

In communicating business results with JHQ, the American president often lacks responsibility, although he is held accountable. As a collaborator, the Japanese VP actively supports the formal position of the American president by playing a leadership role in communicating with JHQ. During the meetings, he complained to the Japanese VP that 'this is not something I made though' during the presentation. The Japanese VP was unhappy with this comment by claiming 'that is not right'. He reveals:

> That is not right . . . that's why I sent him the presentation deck in advance by telling him, please present it, and let me know if you are happy with it or not . . . you present it, meaning this is your presentation . . . I would not tell others that I did it although everybody knows that I did it . . . [but] the top person is not me but him . . .

He attempts to delegate the formal authority to report to JHQ so that both can share the same responsibilities in practice. In the formal presentation, the Japanese VP does not present any part of the material and remains an observer. He, of course, answers questions about the business and the parts of the materials for which he is responsible. What frustrates him is the lack of active participation on the part of the American president, echoing his cultural interpretation of Japan and America.

The American president is aware of his ceremonial position. He, in fact, consulted the American VP about this 'odd' thing and understood that it is a typical practice of Japanese management. Responding to a question about his role, he notes his weakness in understanding Japanese management practices, commenting:

> In my role as President and from my background in Finance and Administration, I understand fairly well my weakness in certain areas of the business. This is why when I took the position as President back in 2008 – I expressed my need to have strong people in key roles within the company, especially in the sales and marketing areas for product sales/strategy, and in operations/ quality for product production in the US.

This comment demonstrates that he is aware of a lack of sales and marketing experience in order to become a president in JUSA. He could not communicate in Japanese so this automatically means that Japanese expatriates need to take the role of communicating with JHQ and with the Japanese contacts at Japanese customers' sites. Indeed, before JUSA, he had never worked or dealt with Japanese MNCs. He had formerly worked as an accountant at an American accounting firm and as a management controller at several American corporations. Thus, it is understandable, as he murmured in the interview, that 'I am not like [the current Japanese VP], nor am I an expatriate from JHQ.' His ceremonial position is closely associated with his profile of not only an inability to communicate in Japanese but also a lack of prior experience of working with Japanese MNCs.

In response to the American president who is unfamiliar with Japanese management practices, the American VP plays an important role as a member of organisational communities spanning boundaries between Japanese family and Western market logics. Reflecting on his long working experience in several large Japanese manufacturers in the United States, he often helps the American president by filling gaps between Japanese and American corporations. He characterised his American president as follows:

> The President that we have is really an accountant person and he was made President because there was no one else to be made President a long time ago and he says that himself. So I'm not saying a bad thing about him, he realizes his gap. But he also realizes that he does not have that type of capability.

According to him, the American president lacks the capability of not only sales and marketing functions but also an understanding of Japanese management practices. Thus, the American VP asserts that 'I am being Japanese to my American boss' to span the boundaries between Japanese and American corporations.

For example, in response to a question of a symbolic role of Japanese expatriates, he advised the American president by drawing on his first-hand experience in several Japanese MNCs. He characterises the role of Japanese expatriates as a coordinator by saying '[the headquarters in Japanese MNCs, in general] tend to have somebody from Japan assigned to the president, kind of like a coordinator'. Indeed, he plays a role in the organisational communities by 'being Japanese' despite that he is not an expatriate from JHQ but a local employee.

The American VP seems to be a strong believer in a philosophical aspect of Japanese management practices. In his private room, he posts his motto for business operations, which he got in working at the former Japanese MNCs. It is written in Japanese, but translates into English as:

Targets:

- Hope is not results but wishful thinking, and therefore needs to be examined.
- Hope is not action.
- Refrain from putting hope into action but move to planned actions.
- Action should be taken without wishful thinking.

He says to me that he strongly believes in the idea of turning wishful thinking into planned actions instead of simply having it. Thus, he tends to be cautious when putting hoped-for business goals into concrete actions to achieve these goals.

In line with his belief in Japanese management practices, he plays a key role of spanning boundaries, as was addressed when initiating the QC activities. He occasionally has to convince the American president of its importance because the president tends to be dead set against sharing management information with those 'lower down on the totem pole', as an American internal sales operator characterises. The American VP recalls the president's attitude of the 'American way, to me, no good reason'. He describes:

Gross profit, so, our cost versus our pricing. [The American president is] concerned about that and I understand everyone who we share data with must control. So I understand his side for that, but I am convincing him that, you know, I expect managers at lower levels from me to control and have power and if I see something already too late that they should have seen first . . .

The American VP has worked at Japanese manufacturers in the United States for more than 12 years, so he is familiar with the family norm. In the interviews with local employees, he was the only one who answered '[JUSA] is an American company. . . . But it is transitioning to a Japanese company . . . that is my view'. When characterising Japanese MNCs, he always refers back to his personal experience in the past at two large Japanese automotive manufacturers. He helps to resolve potential conflict between family and market logics through his career profile constructed within Japanese MNCs and American corporations, manifesting possible institutional reflexivity (Suddaby et al., 2012). In fact, this sharing of information goes along well with the intimate family relationship of Japanese management (e.g. Hatvany and Pucik, 1981; Keys and Miller, 1984).

8.4 Communicating locals' complaints: extended boundaries of organisational communities

Communication about the complaints of the locals creates an extended family to local employees, making the work organisation ceremonial. In JapanCo group, it has been common for some locals to communicate their complaints to top management in JHQ, bypassing their direct managers or directors. In general, the complaint is first made over the heads of subsidiaries to management executives at JHQ, with whom local actors get along. Here, the boundaries of family are considered to be extended to the JapanCo group as a whole, as in a Japanese small firm (Kondo, 1990).

Here, Japanese family logic shapes the sharing of the same information and responsibilities beyond the hierarchy. This refers to a communication style rooted in JHQ, in Japan. Sharing the same information and responsibilities is common in JHQ in which the employee's voice is constantly gathered. There is a voice-gathering system in JHQ: a suggestion box, *ryoshin no koe* ('voice of conscience'). It functions as a contact point for employee opinions, possibly disrupting the organisational hierarchy, as in the subsidiaries. This email box is located in the intra website in Japan and written in Japanese, and directly leads to the CEO of the JapanCo group. This system is expected to incorporate whistleblowing from inside JHQ, although it is not paralleled in the subsidiaries. It also represents 'active participation' in all matters, however. It promotes employee participation as family member engagement, while at the same time allowing the indictment of workplace issues. It enacts collective responsibility and the active participation of the family logic as opposed to the organisational hierarchy.

In the subsidiaries, this system is strongly echoed in local complaints directly communicated with JHQ. Apparently, the local employees are often encouraged to make contact with JHQ. When visiting the subsidiaries, the top management from JHQ tend to remark that local employees are allowed to contact them directly over the heads of subsidiaries. A Japanese manager in JTHAI comments:

> This engineering director and another [from JHQ], visiting [JTHAI], told the locals to possibly contact him by themselves when necessary. In short, it means that it is possible for the locals to contact [JHQ].

For Japanese, this does not mean that local employees can ignore the line of command and control, however. Contacting JHQ can be allowed for reporting important and urgent issues regarding sales activities only, such as adjusting delivery dates and quality problems. For non-Japanese, the comment of the engineering director results in unintentionally encouraging local employees to communicate complaints with JHQ beyond their direct Japanese managers. He elaborates:

> It did not mean that they can disrupt or ignore the chain of command within a subsidiary. For instance, a case can be that a customer's delivery date is severe so there is a need to help to shorten delivery time. Normally, Japanese would understand that this contact [with directors] can be used only for operational purpose but locals would not . . . they would say, they were told to do so, this is why they did it [contacted JHQ].

For Japanese, contacting JHQ manifests Japanese family logic of sharing information for business purposes. This also implies the actors' 'active participation' to gain and maintain the family membership (Kondo, 1990). Meanwhile, local employees feel encouraged to contact JHQ, eventually becoming members of organisational communities. This results in making Japanese expatriates ceremonial managers in the subsidiaries because the locals contacted JHQ over the heads of Japanese expatriates.

   A good illustration of local complaints to JHQ is at JTHAI. A Thai male director and female manager resisted the authoritative and directive actions of a Japanese expatriate by claiming that they suffered 'power harassment' and 'sexual harassment'. Their request was to replace him with another Japanese expatriate as well as to prevent him from coming to one of offices. They directly sent email over the heads of the subsidiaries to the division director at the headquarters who managed the Japanese expatriate by whom they are harassed. As a researcher, I had difficulties interviewing this event in depth with the Thai manager and director in question because they were not prone to talk about this event. The large part of interpretation of complaints rests on a Japanese manager who was complained about. His account was:

> Hearing about the detailed claim of email later, I found that I seem to have been so hard on local sales, and told not to come again [the office in] Rayong, although I had regularly visited the office by week before. So their request to the headquarters was not to let me come to Rayong anymore. I was not mad in front of them but, well, was little bit. More than that, I said, when a local salesman gave a lousy and poor excuse of losing sales opportunity, it is wrong and unacceptable. I was not convinced of the excuse so I told them that I need to interview with him. I was told not to do so by them.

The compliant manifests a conflict between family responsibilities of raising subordinates and the benevolence of leaders believed in Theravada Buddhism. The Japanese expatriate interprets his role as to show anger to correct his employee's shortcomings, while the Thais rather prioritise the religious mindset to forgive them (see 7.2). The contacts at JHQ are normally management executives who recognised the local employees. According to the Japanese expatriate, the source of the complaint concerns the religious merits of forgiveness, which has to be shared among JHQ for their own interest. That is, he got angry with the Thai salesperson who did not seriously pursue sales opportunities. In front of members in a meeting, he got angry although he knew that showing anger in public is not accepted in Thai society. He even commented in Japanese that 'someone needs to scold local employees so that the Thais can get better . . . so I am taking this role of showing anger'. He expects to raise his Thais as he did in Japan.

The Japanese expatriate firmly believes that anger is somewhat necessary to raise his Thai subordinates through family logic (see 7.2). For his view, he may have seen opportunities to treat and raise his men as his 'child'. Nonetheless, Thai employees see constraints in terms of their religious belief in benevolence derived from Theravada Buddhism. Both actors' view a manifest competitive relationship between Japanese family and Thai Buddhism. This complaint, however, is somewhat puzzling for him because this was not the first time he got angry. He explains the source of this embarrassment:

> In the email, I am supposed to have sexually harassed her. I have known her for 10 years and invited her to my home party. I have gotten in with her for long term but I did not understand why she suddenly claimed this. . . . Never until this time had I been complained by them although I have been working with them for 7 years. This is the first time that they resisted. I really do not understand. Anger? Probably, yes.

Reacting with surprise to this unexpected complaint, he reflects on what he has done with Thais and realised that his display of anger seemed to cause their resistance. Showing anger is against religious merit, benevolence and forgiveness, thereby provoking the locals' complaints.

The profile of the Japanese expatriate is closely linked to the JapanCo group. He began his career with JapanCo in Japan and has worked approximately 30 years. He has worked at JTHAI for seven years, which is his first experience of being an expatriate. He further comments that 'Japanese in Asia tend to be respected' because of their outstanding historical and economic development in comparison with Asian countries. Thailand has been invested in by Japanese manufacturers as the hub in Asia. Taiwan, as another example, had been under Japan rule and thus 'Japanese tend to be welcomed', as a Japanese expatriate in JTAIW mentions. In addition, a series of his comments parallels the notion of Asia in Japanese minds as the former Japanese expatriate MD in Asia and Europe comments that:

> [in my tenancy at subsidiaries] I found Japanese expatriates tend to communicate very differently with local employees, according to the employees, either Western or Asian. . . . With Asians, a terrible attitude, they look down [Asians] and say like, why don't you listen to me? . . . I did not like that . . .

For Japanese expatriates, the hierarchy means that Japan is above Asia, yet below the West. This notion of Asia is consistent with the view of the Japanese expatriate in JTHAI. He justifies why Japanese expatriates, including himself, are necessary in JTHAI by mentioning that 'Japanese expatriates need to be here, as change leaders'. He referred back to the historical fact that a Japanese soldier named Yamada Nagamasa became a governor in Thailand during the seventeenth century. He reasoned that talented foreigners like Japanese, therefore, are always crucial to maintain a favorable Thai society.

In the case here, the family norm may have been instrumental for the Thais in raising their complaints to JHQ. After the complaint ended, the Japanese manager, resisted by locals through headquarters, laments that there is no rule of communication between the headquarters and local employees. He continues to describe how JHQ reacts to this resistance.

> The Japan side, while not knowing locals much, tends to take all the credits for local employees without questioning. It tends to have great affection for the locals, and then, and goes on to criticize Japanese expatriates by saying what are you doing? This makes all the expatriates working hard overseas useless.

The contacts in JHQ are top management directors and vice presidents. When receiving complaints from local employees, who are mostly young, they often take for granted the locals' complaints without scrutiny. The family norm may have been utilised for bringing the Thais' complaint. Both the Thai director and manager have worked at JTHAI for more than 10 years, yet had no prior working experience with Japanese MNCs. Neither have they worked outside Thailand. Their profiles strongly imply that the Thais strategically deploy the boundary of a whole family, including the subsidiaries, through their active participation while downplaying the organisational hierarchy.

8.5 Discussions and conclusion

This chapter explores how work organisation practices are interpreted through ceremonial aspects and how actors in turn are organised. The finding of this chapter is that the boundaries of the organisational communities are not simply segmented to Japanese expatriates but constructed through the actors' profiles. The finding elaborates on the receptivity of 'intraorganisational communities', which is supposed to affect the given meaning of logics in the subsidiaries. Greenwood et al. (2011) argue that the receptivity may be strongly affected by 'the thickness of ties' of organisational communities to their organisational fields. At first sight, this seems to support Japanese organisational communities. Japanese expatriates are structured as the dominant organisational community, manifesting *uchi*, the inside group of the ethnocentric family (Kondo, 1990). Indeed, different HR management systems between Japanese expatriates and locals strongly support this Japanese organisational community (see 8.3). The dominant Japanese community can play a role in spanning the boundaries of family members within JapanCo group and its subsidiaries, manifesting the uncontested boundaries of organisational communities. This parallels the intimate relations between logics and the types of actors, geographical communities and organisations that are supposed to be segmented (Goodrick and Reay, 2011).

The receptivity of organisational communities is, however, further constructed by the actors' personal profiles, rather than the actors' positions as structurally defined. This supports the significance of actors' profiles as institutional reflexivity, indicated by Suddaby et al. (2012). In JUSA, the boundaries of the organisational communities are extended to the American VP, not the American president, owing to his career profile of working at several Japanese manufacturers in the past. The American president, despite his leadership position, is separated from organisational communities according to a lack of 'active participation' (Kondo, 1990) (see 8.3). In fact, both the American president and vice-president have different profiles: the former had no working experience with Japanese MNCs, while the latter has extensive experience over a number of decades. The American vice-president, as he says himself, often plays a role of being Japanese toward the American president. In JTHAI, the Thai director and manager who has worked at JTHAI for a long time are aware of the Japanese family within the JapanCo group through their length of service in JTHAI. Their experience of working at other Japanese MNCs turns out to be a key element in playing the role of organisational communities spanning the manifested boundaries between Japanese family and the Western market. Indeed, they play a role of the organisational communities spanning the boundaries between Japanese family and Thai Theravada Buddhism. This indicates the significance of the actors' career profile, of working at Japanese MNCs in this case, which potentially defines a member of the organisational communities. The receptivity of organisational communities (Greenwood et al., 2011) can be constructed mostly through the actors' career profiles, especially in terms of experiencing different Japanese MNCs in this case.

Perhaps, in the cases examined here, actors with their career profiles of working at only one corporation can be deeply embedded in their original environments. Both the Japanese VP in JUSA and the Japanese expatriate in JTHAI are examples. The Japanese VP in JUSA, who began his career and never had expatriate experience before, firmly believes that Americans need to be above Japanese expatriates because of historical development in respect to Japan that 'we [Japanese] are underneath [the United States] so it would cause conflicts when Japanese try to take a leadership role, however, it would go well when an American is assigned as a leader'. Furthermore, the Japanese expatriate in JTHAI, who had spent his entire career in JapanCo, firmly believes that he needs to be a leader toward his Thai subordinates whenever necessary. He is actively taking a role of scolding his Thais whenever necessary by saying that 'Japanese expatriates need to be here, as change leaders' referencing the historical figure, Yamada Nagamasa, who was a successful Japanese governor in seventeenth-century Thailand. This further implies that the actors' profiles of having worked at one institutional environment manifests a particular logic that may be further embedded in their 'life history' rather than having institutional reflexivity (Battilana and Dorado,

2010; Suddaby et al., 2012). It questions the structurally pre-set 'organisational communities' through an 'organisational filter' (Greenwood et al., 2011).

8.6 Personal reflection: overhead diplomacy and unwelcoming Japanese expatriates in their host countries

Overhead diplomacy within Japanese MNCs is not unusual. The source of this type of problem is a strong emphasis on the family norm of sharing all the information whether it is good or bad. Local employees often to perceive that their voice can be heard through social events with those from the headquarters in Japan. Then, whenever bad things happen to them, they make contact with those at the headquarters with whom they are acquainted. Management executives upon receiving complaints from them tend to actively involve themselves in finding solutions to these complaints. They act as judges to decide whether these occurrences are right or not, without knowing full well what happened in local subsidiaries. Ironically, the Japanese executives themselves destroy their organisational hierarchies in a local subsidiary under the family norm. For local employees, open communication, albeit in Japanese does not mean a flat organisation, but may be strongly associated with the concept of family without organisational hierarchies. Perhaps, managers collecting information and hearing their workers' voices are seen as weak and naïve in some countries' contexts.

There was also an incident that the Japanese MD in JTHAI previously experienced as the president of a Japanese subsidiary in the United States. His female manager, who was not performing well, made a direct complaint to his boss, the CEO at the headquarters of the company. Indeed, the CEO heard her complaint and reacted by asking him what happened to her in the United States. He rather openly became defiant and told his CEO that 'you can judge both of us to decide which one is right'. However, the CEO came to a judgement, trusting her over him, despite the fact that it was the CEO who assigned and dispatched him to the United States in the first place. Then, the Japanese president in the United States eventually resigned because, as he said, 'I could no longer manage my business given the fact that my subordinate's complaint is prioritised over what I said to the CEO.' This is probably a specific issue to Japanese MNCs while not in the Western corporations where overhead diplomacy is formally prohibited. I remember my colleague's story that while working at an American subsidiary in Japan, he tried to report some incident to a director, a boss of his direct one. It was because he was frustrated with his direct boss neither hearing what was happening in the sales fields nor being aware of the importance of the incident. He thought that he could be heard, however, the director rejected the request of a meeting with him because of their corporate rule. Under the rule, it was not allowed to receive a formal report from subordinates at a lower grade, especially two grades below, than one's own grade. This meant that my colleague was not allowed to make a formal report to the director.

Between Japanese, I found that even this overhead communication is praised and practiced under the name of employee voice meetings. At one of the large American consulting firms in Japan where almost all employees are Japanese, their Japanese president regularly holds meetings with the freshmen who enter the firm every year. This town meeting is an occasion where the president not only receives information about their workplace but also fires incompetent managers based on comments and feedback from freshmen in the meeting. There were cases where some managers were so badly reported by the freshmen that they suffered harsh words or were allocated extra hard work. After one meeting, the Japanese president immediately called a meeting with a manager and fired him. My colleague disclosed, while laughing, that this meeting was called internally as 'trial and execution of managers'. Later on, I heard that he left the firm but I am not sure of whether he was fired or not.

A series of events regarding direct complaints makes organisational hierarchy meaningless and eventually ceremonial. Organisational charts in local subsidiaries often manifest the ceremonial and ethnocentric characters of Japanese MNCs. In a large Japanese automotive manufacturer in the United States, I found that Japanese expatriates are rarely assigned as line managers, but rather as advisors who are free from the business line. In their organisational charts where boxes and lines explain command and control, the boxes of Japanese expatriates are lined next to local managers or sometimes two names, Japanese and the local, in one box. Therefore, they both share their roles although the Japanese are not directly responsible for the business. They are evaluated not by the local director or managers but by Japanese expatriates within a Japanese network separated from the local one, as discussed in this chapter. From time to time, they are not welcome and thus treated by the locals in an unfriendly manner. It is a known fact that some Japanese expatriates cannot wait to finish their assignment and return home to Japan. Every day, they are counting the days on a calendar on their desks until the day when they can go back to their home country. This may be another issue in managing Japanese expatriates in international business.

9 Discussion and conclusion

9.1 Summary of the findings

The purpose of this research is to explore how practices are interpreted differently across the foreign subsidiaries of a Japanese MNC. An institutional logic approach was adopted, with a focus on the constellations of logics. Categories of practices across the subsidiaries of JapanCo emerged inductively through a quasi-ethnographic study. These practices relate to customer development, work and employment, and work organisation. The key findings of the study concern the relevance of culture, context and ceremonial features for the operation of institutional logics. The significance of culture is appreciated, chiefly through cooperative relationships, but especially among the family and religion logics. The significance of context is assessed through the competitive relationships among contextual enactments of logics. Finally, ceremonial aspects are illuminated through cooperative as well as competitive logics. Each finding is elaborated as follows.

First, the significance of a national culture is assessed through the cooperative relationships between logics (see chapter 6). Two findings are identified; both of them concern the significance of a national culture. First, the family norm of Japanese culture and Thai Theravada Buddhism are manifested through practices. In particular, Japanese family are enacted in Japanese customer development (see 6.2), such as on-the-job training and study groups for salespeople. The Thai manager tends to ascribe the family to a Japanese model, which is based on reciprocity and obligation. In JTHAI, *oyabun kobun* and *senpai* are expressed as Japanese family members while *ongaeshi* is the burden of the child (see 6.3). The child, once grown up, is obligated to return favours to the parents. This responsibility has little to do with 'unconditional loyalty' as such, prioritising more 'reciprocity and obligation rather than obedience (Bhappu, 2000)'. This obligation is based on *ko* and *on* relationships within the Japanese family, enabling study group and on-the-job training for Thai salespeople during non-working hours. Furthermore, it also entails an expanded concept of the family, including non-blood relationships; whereas the Western family usually means direct blood relationships in the nuclear family. In on-the-job training and study groups, even subordinates are included as family members because they characterise themselves as 'we are "family'. The notion of the Japanese family can coexist with the corporation and still manifest the host country's culture. This finding highlights the significance of a national culture as the medium through which practices are interpreted.

Moreover, these helping practices and relationships are also manifested in Theravada Buddhism (see 6.4). Unlike Christianity, Theravada Buddhism promotes the attainment of religious merits through the act of helping others and benevolence, in preference to sacredness. In Theravada Buddhism, a leader is expected to be a benevolent father who is tolerant of the mistakes of others and accepting of things as they are. For example, in job delegation, the Thai director performed the job as an act of benevolence instead of delegating it to his incapable subordinates. He never scolded, although Japanese often do, or got upset in front of others; generally smiling and saying, '*Mai pen rai*' ('never mind') (see 6.4). Even in socialisation, the Thais tended to go out and have dinner and lunch together, and have Japanese expatriates pay for the bill without offering their thanks, manifesting religious merit where the 'haves' help the 'have-nots'. Both Japanese family and Theravada Buddhism are intertwined through the actors' cultural interpretations, thus strengthening each other.

Second, in JTHAI, both the Japanese family norm and Theravada Buddhism amplify each other (see 6.2., 6.3). Here, the Thai employees in JTHAI are motivated to be family members who cooperate through seniority (the corporation), helping each other to ultimately gain religious merit (religion) as well as improved economic results (market). For the Thai employees, 'company as "family"' is expressed through their identification with JTHAI, and by showing their benevolence in Theravada Buddhism by helping others and forgiving others' mistakes. The Thai managers and directors spend their non-working hours instructing their employees. They volunteer to form study groups to teach their employees how to deal with Japanese customers. The relationships among logics are strengthened as well as facilitated, manifesting in amplified relationships.

Third, the significance of context is assessed through the competitive relationships between logics (see chapter 7). Another finding was that the constellations of logics are ongoing and continuously formed in relation to geographical locations. Actors' negotiations and conflicts continue in order to solve competitive relationships among logics. Both bonus and sales incentives enact multiple logics, eventually generating competitive relationships among logics. In JTHAI, for example, Thai employees find opportunities to manifest religious merit by forgiving others' mistakes when pursuing sales opportunities with Japanese expatriates, manifesting a tension between religion and market logics (see 7.2). Job delegation enacts a tension between self-improvement (family), self-acceptance (religion) and self-interest (market). This tension demonstrates the situatedness of actors, because some see opportunities while others see constraints within the same practices. In another instance at JTHAI, the Japanese family, as enacted by Thais asserting that 'we are family', conflicts with Theravada Buddhism in respect to bill payment (see 7.4.1). In addition, it conflicts with the market efficiency expected by the Japanese MD. This stems from the notion that constellations of logics are dynamic and ongoing processes of enacting logics.

Moreover, the constellations of logics are to some extent different in Asia and the West. For example, in Asia, such as at JTHAI and JTAIW, family logic is enacted through the employment practices (see 7.3.1; 7.4.1): the local employees treat bonuses as a collective reward, prioritising group performance over individual performance. In particular, in JTHAI, social events are active and there are even company trips and parties. By contrast, market logic in JUSA is strongly enacted by performance appraisal and socialisation (see 7.3.2; 7.4.2). Sales incentives and promotions are interpreted as individual rewards, and no bonus is adopted. There are few social events, which are considered a means to keep independent professional relationships to a bare minimum, rather than building a family norm, as in JTHAI.

However, geographical location does not solely determine the constellations of logics. Some Thais and Taiwanese insist on an increase in individual salary (see 7.3.1), while an American director wants JUSA to become a Japanese company. These examples demonstrate nuanced articulations of constellations of logics in their geographical locations. As Abo (2015) and Lounsbury (2007) point out, geographical locations matter. This finding also highlights the significance of context, such as surrounding environments as well as the geographical locations where practices are conducted, as other institutionalists have recently argued (e.g. Goodrick and Reay, 2011; Delbridge and Edwards, 2013).

Fourth, the ceremonial aspects are assessed through the constellations of logics (see chapter 8). Indeed, the boundaries of organisational communities are not 'segmented' to Japanese expatriates but extended through the actors' profiles. This raises the significance of the actors' profile in having institutional reflexivity (Suddaby et al., 2012) and echoes the contested meanings of family, as Kondo (1990) asserts. At first sight, Japanese expatriates are structurally constructed as the dominant organisational community by the organisational field (Greenwood et al., 2011), manifesting *uchi*, or the inside group of the ethnocentric family. The different HR management systems between Japanese expatriates and locals strongly support this Japanese organisational community, echoing 'two management structures' (Elger and Smith, 2005) (see 8.2). Indeed, the dominant Japanese community plays a role spanning the boundaries of family members within the JapanCo group and its subsidiaries.

In practice, however, the boundaries of the organisational communities are due largely to the actors' profiles of whether they have intensive working experience at Japanese MNCs. In particular, in JUSA, the American president has little previous working experience with Japanese MNCs, while the American VP has intensive experience over several decades (see 8.3). The American VP says that he plays the role of 'being Japanese' toward the American president by promoting Japanese management practices, such as sharing information in the QC circle. He has extensive work experience at several large Japanese MNCs and expertise in Japanese management practices, especially on the manufacturing side. His career profile, albeit not as a Japanese expatriate in JUSA, allows him actively to play a role in organisational communities that connect themselves to Japanese management practices that are possibly conduced in JHQ. Being Japanese, he often convinces the American VP of how the headquarters in Japanese MNCs manage to establish subsidiaries by dispatching Japanese expatriates who are expected to play the role of coordinator. Based on extensive working experience at Japanese MNCs, the actors' profiles may help to play the role of organisational communities that construct and conduct Japanese management practices manifesting family logic. In contrast, the American president stays separated from the organisational communities due to his lack of 'active participation' (Kondo, 1990) (see 8.2). These accounts elaborate on the simple notion of having dominant Japanese expatriates (Westney, 1987; 1999). Here, the boundaries of the organisational communities are constructed through the actors' profiles in addition to their active participation.

9.2 Theoretical contributions

Drawing on the findings previously reviewed, four main theoretical contributions are identified: cultural effects on logics; amplification of logics; ongoing constellations of logics; and actors' profile in organisational communities.

First, in chapter 6, the finding that the cooperative relationships between family and religion logics are culturally embodied by the practices in customer development highlights the serious limitations of the institutional logic approach, which is based on Western society (Thornton et al., 2012). In Japanese family logic, reciprocity and obligation are strongly assumed among family members. This shows a sharp contrast to the 'unconditional loyalty' in Western society (Thornton et al., 2012). Both Japanese and Western logics have in common family logic, but the legitimacies of these logics are different and thus potentially enable different actors' behaviours.

A Japanese family is governed by reciprocal *ko* and *on* relationships (Kondo, 1990; Bhappu, 2000), rather than the unconditional loyalty that legitimates the Western family, according to Thornton et al. (2012). This difference originates from the importance of the 'reproduction of "family" members' as Friedland and Alford (1991) state. This Western family logic seems to be consistent with Western family firms (e.g. Karra et al., 2006). The Japanese family, however, is governed by reciprocity and obligation as Bhappu (2000) argues. *Oyabun kobun* and *senpai* are expressed as a burden of Japanese family members. *Ongaeshi* is

Table 9.1 Comparison of legitimacies of logics (Thornton et al., 2012) and cultural interpretations

Logics	Its legitimacies (Thornton et al., 2012)	Cultural interpretations
Family logic	Unconditional loyalty	Reciprocity and obligation (Japanese family)
Religion logic	Sacredness in economy	Religious merit (Thai Theravada Buddhism)

repayment to those whom one thinks it is owed. The child, especially after maturing, is obligated to return favours to the parents. This meaning of family is also influenced by Japan's collectivistic society (Hofstede, 2010). Here, it has little to do with unconditional loyalty, prioritising more 'reciprocity and obligation rather than obedience' (Bhappu, 2000). It is also not consistent with the parental altruism that can manifest in Western family firms (e.g. Karra et al., 2006; Nordqvist and Melin, 2010).

Moreover, Theravada Buddhism is strongly manifested through cultural interpretation of religious merits. A leader in Theravada Buddhism is expected to be a benevolent father. This contrasts with the religion logic based on Christianity's governed 'sacredness' (Thornton et al., 2012). Although Thornton *et al.* reworked the religion logic to be universal rather than Christian, their definition is still a residue from Christianity, rather than incorporating other religious viewpoints such as Theravada Buddhism. These parallel potential limitations have already been pointed out by Friedland and Alford (1991), who remind us of the importance of the differences between Western and non-Western societies. The family and religion logics are deeply rooted in geographical communities (Marquis and Lounsbury, 2007) in Japan and Thailand. This strongly echoes the 'cultural space' for which categorical elements of logics may compete as Thornton et al. (2012) remind us of the organisational field structure as favouring conditions of particular logics. The finding illuminates that 'cultural space' in non-Western society, such as Asia, is composed of fundamentally different elements of family and religion logics. This further questions the universality of the framework, which is implicitly assumed in their arguments. The elements of institutional logics may not be universally applicable.

Second, in chapter 6, the finding that both Japanese family and Theravada Buddhism strengthen each other directly supports the presupposition of amplification itself (Greenwood et al., 2010; 2011) while elaborating the facilitative relationship among logics that simply guide practices without conflicts (Goodrick and Reay, 2011). In this study, the Thai employees in JTHAI are motivated to be family members (the family) who cooperate through seniority (the corporation) and help each other (the religion) to ultimately gain economic results (the market). All of these logics are not only facilitating but also amplifying; strengthening themselves in other words. This is consistent with what Greenwood et al. (2010) showed to be the relationship between Spanish family-owned firms and Catholicism. It also confirms Bhappu's (2000) identification of family and religion logics within Japanese MNCs. She demonstrates the existence of the family and religion logic simply operating within Japanese MNCs, but fails to point out how these logics coexist and cooperate. Logics are likely to amplify each other through the meanings of reciprocity. At the same time, this amplified relationship proves to be distinctive from the facilitative relationship in the sense of strengthening logics although Waldorff, Reay, and Goodrick (2013) treat the amplified relationship as facilitative. This further implies that a possible condition favouring amplified relationships may be deeply concerned with the actors' cultural interpretation.

Similarly, this casts further doubt on the current literature that examines how practices are executed across the subsidiaries of Japanese MNCs. It might be amplification with other logics rather than simple Japanisation that intensifies the family norm. Reflecting on the current literature which focuses on the industry level (e.g. Oliver and Wilkinson, 1993), Japanese management scholars may have failed to articulate the amplified effects of family and other logics, in favour of a simplistically dominant family logic. In particular, this applies to some Japanese MNCs in Thailand in the sense that 'Thai workers were seen to be more familiar and comfortable with the collectivist orientation of Japanese managers (Atmiyanandana and Lawler, 2003, p. 238)' than the managers in the Western MNCs. It might have been initially recognised as Japanisation enacted by dominant family yet, on closer examination, family is amplified by multiple plural logics through cultural interpretations as demonstrated in this chapter.

Third, there is one theoretical significance of the finding in chapter 7 that the constellations of logics are ongoing and continuously formed in relation to geographical locations. This finding contrasts with the institutionalists' strong focus on a static competition between two logics that can be relatively easily described and explained by clear solutions such as segmenting (Goodrick and Reay, 2011) or compartmentalisation (Greenwood et al., 2011). Here, contextually enacted logics do not necessarily lead to victory or defeat for lengthy periods in practice, but are rather being continuously formed. In this research, neither segmenting nor compartmentalisation were evident as means to mediate the competitive relationship. This questions the simple notion of 'winner' or 'loser' logics (Thornton, 2004) and blended logics (Thornton et al., 2012), as well as 'organisational filter' and 'field level structure' possibly determining the actors' actions (Greenwood et al., 2011). Instead, the actors make relationships competitive according to the contexts in which they conduct practices.

Furthermore, the finding possibly negates the concept of 'segmenting', which aims to separate the impacts of logics on different actors, geographical communities and organisations to solve the conflicts caused by competitive relationships (Goodrick and Reay, 2011). Here, actors are situated in their contexts so some see opportunities while others see constraints within the same practices on an ongoing basis. Therefore, constellations of logics – i.e. more than two logics – are not automatically formed as a result of societal effects or 'organisational filters' but are created by actors in contexts (Delbridge and Edwards, 2007; 2013). This further elaborates on the situatedness of actors (e.g. Delbridge and Edwards, 2013) in a more nuanced manner. The need for relational institutional analysis has long been argued by Delbridge and Edwards (2007) and has recently been taken into account for two logics (e.g. Smets and Jarzabkowski, 2013).

In addition, the finding reveals the serious limitation of the feasibility of the organisational filter that Greenwood et al. (2011) propose. This notion of a given and pre-set 'organisational filter' and the abstract, top down effect of institutional logic, is not sufficient to explore the institutional complexity within practices, thus questioning the notion of complexity filtered by organisational attributes

(Greenwood et al., 2011). The notion of an organisational filter and attributes may lead to the reifying of organisations as abstract entities, thereby neglecting the dynamic processes of building complexity, as demonstrated in this research. This shows that actors make relationships competitive according to the contexts in which they conduct the practices.

Moreover, the finding that the constellations of logics are different in Asia and the West highlights the importance of the geographical communities where logics are rooted (Lounsbury, 2007). In Asia, family logic is enacted through employment practices. In JTHAI and JTAIW, actors treat bonuses as a collective reward. This echoes the work of Abo (2015) who argues for how geographical locations may influence Japanese management practice. In contrast, in the West, market logic is strongly enacted by performance appraisal and socialisation. A sales incentive and promotion are interpreted as individual reward while no bonus is adopted. This explains the work of Elger and Smith (1994; 2005), illuminating how Japanese management practices are rejected and resisted. Although the geographical locations are deeply associated with the enactment of competitive logics, these never determine the relationships among them as the situatedness of actors is discussed (e.g. Delbridge and Edwards, 2013; Smets and Jarzabkowski, 2013).

In addition, by focusing on the plural logics normally discussed by institutionalists, this chapter advances the constellations of institutional logics (Goodrick and Reay, 2011) by taking into account how these plural logics interact continually. Logics are not restricted to only two competitive ones but to plural ones according to the actors in context. The chapter also elaborates on the situatedness of the actors (e.g. Delbridge and Edwards, 2013; Smets and Jarzabkowski, 2013) in a more nuanced manner, confirming the need for the kind of 'relational institutional analysis' that Delbridge and Edwards (2007) argue for. Conversely, the family norm is strategically utilised by the Thai director who wants to share jobs efficiently. Practices can be due to 'both intentional and unintentional outcomes' in the 'everyday getting by of individuals' (Lawrence et al., 2011) according to the relational contexts in which actors conduct practices. After all, constellations of logics and institutional complexity need to be treated as a dynamic and ongoing process of enacting institutional logics as other constellations of logics.

Finally, there is theoretical significance of the finding in chapter 8 that the boundaries of the organisational communities are not segmented to Japanese expatriates but constructed through the actors' profiles. This finding raises the importance of the actors' profiles supporting a possible institutional reflexivity, as Suddaby et al. (2012) point out. They raise the significance of 'variations in one's personal biography' which is composed of 'their social position, their educational history, their network relationships' (Suddaby et al., 2012, p. 13). These substantial individual differences among actors are important in this research, especially in the Japanese MNCs examined here. Indeed the American VP, albeit not the president, is 'being Japanese' toward the American boss. His career profile in several Japanese MNCs greatly influences his capability to reflect his institutional environments in JTHAI. The American president, however, tends to be in a ceremonial position due to a lack of active participation. In this case, these differences are made by the actors' profiles in respect to their work experience at Japanese MNCs by enacting Japanese family logic. This echoes the work of Battilana and Dorado (2010) who raise the importance of the actors' profiles when exposed to some practices enacting a particular logic. They indicate that the actors' life history may be fundamental to playing the role of organisational community members. The institutionalists' normally focus on the macro- and meso-level studies in adopting quantitative methods, eventually failing to grasp (e.g. Thornton et al., 2012) the 'substantial individual differences' among actors (Suddaby et al., 2012). It also questions a simple articulation of the receptivity of organisational communities, which can be strongly affected by 'the thickness of ties' to their organisational fields (Greenwood et al., 2011). With the actors' suitable career profiles, they can play a role of organisational communities regardless of whether they are structurally defined as members of organisational communities connecting their organisational fields.

In addition, the finding further questions organisational communities as structurally defined by their organisational fields, as Greenwood et al (2011) argue. The boundaries of family can be contested with the actors' 'active participation' (Kondo, 1990) and their profile. In theory, Japanese expatriates can be structurally entitled to be the organisational community to connect themselves to JHQ, as Greenwood et al. (2011) argue that the 'intraorganisational communities' are supposed to be structurally defined by connecting themselves to the organisational fields. In practice, however, much like the American VP being Japanese and the Thai director and manager, actors are able to play a role of organisational communities connecting to JHQ, or their fields in other words. This also throws doubt on the intimate relationship between logics and types of actors, geographical communities and organisations (Goodrick and Reay, 2011). The boundaries of organisational communities are dynamically constructed rather than defined by their fields. These accounts develop a more nuanced articulation of the contested boundaries of organisational communities (Greenwood et al., 2011).

9.3 Implications for managers

This research provides several practical implications for managers, regardless of whether they are Japanese working at Japanese MNCs. Managers should understand actors' cross-cultural interpretations of practices; they should pay attention to the contexts of tensions between Japanese and locals; they should be aware of ceremonial aspects in two management structures; and they should understand the significance of the actors' profile of boundary spanners.

First, managers should understand the cross-cultural interpretations of practices with a host country culture (see chapters 6, 7 and 8). The same practice can be interpreted differently through actors' cultural interpretations of a host and home country culture. In this research, typical practices for Japanese MNCs are identified, such as on-the-job training, study groups, luncheon meetings, QC control, philosophy, sharing practices, socialisation and communication with JHQ and customers locally. Through these practices, actors differentially 'inhabit' meanings of logics and culture. In JTHAI, the Thai employees characterise the company as family while gaining religious merit by helping others (see 6.3, 6.4, 7.3.1, 7.4.1, 8.4). Both the family norm and Theravada Buddhism can be intertwined, thus enabling the same actions on the part of actors: helping others and forgiving others' mistakes (see 6.4). Indeed, some Japanese expatriates particularly admire the Thais for these actions, recognising them as those of the Japanese family. Others attribute them to the Thai religion, Theravada Buddhism, thus denying the existence of Japanese family. Even if actors' actions are superficially similar to those of the Japanese, cultural meanings are not necessarily the same as a Japanese observer might think.

Furthermore, this cross-cultural interpretation does not mean that Japanese do things one way while locals act in another fixed manner. In JTHAI, some locals express the importance of the family norm while some Japanese not at all. In addition, there can be local employees who act like Japanese expatriates. For example, in JTHAI, there is a Thai manager who speaks Japanese and emphasises the *oyabun* and *kobun* paternal relationship (see 6.3). In JUSA, an American director is passionate about changing the status of JUSA as American company into a Japanese company where family logic can operate (see 8.3). Here, there is no simple formula as to how Japanese expatriates might act and how local employees in turn react.

Second, managers should pay attention to tensions and conflicts between Japanese and locals through logics (see chapter 7). These tensions and conflicts can be different according to the relational contexts of actors in a geographical location. In Asia, a collectivistic orientation based on family can be enhanced. A bonus manifests a collective reward in relation to their collectivistic orientations. In particular, a Thai manager insists on an increase in salary for her employees by stating that her salary has been raised enough, thus gaining religious merit in respect to Theravada Buddhism. Social events are active and there are even company trips and parties. In contrast, in the West, individualistic economic efficiency based on the market is strongly emphasised by performance appraisal and socialisation. Sales incentives and promotion are interpreted as individual rewards while no bonus is adopted (see 7.3.2). There are few social events, which is a means to keep independent professional relationships to the bare minimum, rather than building the family norm as in JTHAI (see 7.4.2). In Asia and the West, therefore, the types of tensions and conflicts may be different.

The geographical and cultural contexts of Asia and the West do not always determine the competitive relationships among logics. In JTAIW, despite company trips and parties, there seem to be few informal social events: Taiwanese tend not to go out together as at JTHAI. In JTHAI, meanwhile, some Thai employees make an effort to argue for salary increases when assigned sales development jobs acquiring new customers or projects. Furthermore, the American director who had previously worked at large Japanese automotive manufacturers insists that JUSA is an 'American company' now, but that it is going to be Japanese company. Thus, the geographical and cultural contexts are deeply associated with enactment of competitive logics, but do not determine the relationships between them.

Third, managers need to be aware of ceremonial aspects in two management structures within the subsidiaries of Japanese MNCs (see chapter 8). This research shows how 'two management structures' (Elger and Smith, 2005) are constructed through the actors' cultural interpretation and contextual enactment of logics. Initially, it has been reinforced by the dominant role of Japanese expatriates (Westney, 1987; 1999). In communicating expatriate evaluation, two structures are reinforced by the separation between Japanese expatriates and local employees. There are different HR management systems for Japanese expatriates and locals, which causes tension in communicating business results by the American president, bringing about competition between corporation and market logics. These negate the simple notion of having dominant Japanese expatriates (Westney, 1987; 1999), however, and instead support a more nuanced articulation of ceremonial aspects according to the actors in their contexts. Eventually, the two structures are sustained as a ceremonial work organisation norm that is mediated through the collective responsibility of family.

Furthermore, these ceremonial aspects are influenced by Japanese cultural interpretations of the hierarchy between Asia and the West (see 8.3). Although some Thais in JTHAI are promoted as directors above the Japanese, some Thais still consider the Japanese expatriate manager as the boss of the Thai directors because he is Japanese. In the West, the American president was appointed although the Japanese VP is the main contact with JHQ. The Japanese VP firmly believes that, in JUSA, the American president is simply better than the Japanese, owing to the US hierarchical position in the Japanese mentality. These cultural interpretations might shape these ceremonial aspects.

Finally, managers should understand the significance of the actors' profile of boundary spanners between different geographical locations (Suddaby, et al., 2012). The American VP in JUSA has extensive work experience at several large Japanese MNCs over a number of decades. The American VP, as he says himself, tends to play a role of being Japanese toward the American president, eventually playing a role of spanning boundaries between Japanese family and Western market logics. His career profile helps him to understand and span the possible boundaries within MNCs, possibly connecting the foreign subsidiaries to their headquarters. By contrast, the Japanese VP in JUSA is deeply embedded in their original environments in Japan. He never had an expatriate experience before. This strongly implicates the significance of actors' career profile, of working at Japanese MNCs in this case, which potentially defines a member of organisational communities.

9.4 Limitations and future research questions

As with all the institutional studies, this research has several limitations. First, an issue of generalisability may arise because of the comparative ethnographic case studies. Although JapanCo has a long history and has operated for more than a hundred years since its incorporation in Japan, it is just one of many Japanese MNCs, and thus this case may neither represent nor be generalised to the population of Japanese MNCs. It does not help to 'enumerate frequencies', which generalise as 'statistical generalisation'. It does, however, expand the institutional logics approach as 'analytic generalisation' (Yin, 2003), linking findings in specific cases to a theory, which allows the ethnographic approach. Thus, the issue may remain but can be solved by focusing on aspects of expanding theories.

Second, an issue of reliability may arise because of one coder and languages. Data is coded based on a single coder, although this can be alleviated by re-coding. Also, there is a language problem especially in the interviews with Thais, Taiwanese and Belgium, whose first language is not English. In this case, I was reliant more on the Japanese expatriates' accounts than those of the local employees, because some of them did not express themselves well in English. Overall, however, the quasi-ethnography nature of the study with a deep understanding of the data combines with 'thick description' presentations in a way that should be sufficient to address the concerns regarding reliability (Silverman, 2006).

Third, an issue of at-home ethnography may arise because of treating the researcher as the object of the study, which might limit the researcher to the taken-for-granted idea at his home. Alvesson (2009, p. 166) posts a fair warning that '(b)eing personally involved in the object of study (the context in which one is studying) also means that one may be less able to liberate oneself from some taken-for-granted ideas or to view things in an open-minded way'. Although any social research can never be entirely neutral (Burrel and Morgan, 1979), it is possible to be more sensitive to the ideas through careful reflection. Here, reflexivity is actively enhanced throughout the data collection and analysis process.

There are also several future research questions identified in this book. Potential future research concerns the relationships between logics and culture. This research indicates the significance of culture with logics but has not yet elaborated on the relationship between logics and culture. Thornton et al. (2012) briefly touch on 'cultural space' from the institutional logics perspective. Cultural space should matter here, given the research in a non-Western region, such as Asia, as demonstrated in this research. This raises the possibility that there might be another version of institutional logics perspectives in non-Western society, which is distinctive from that of Thornton et al. (2012). In particular, family and religion logics can be further explored, especially in the Asian region.

Another potential research area is regarding agency in constellations of logics. In reference to Suddaby et al. (2012), this research shows the significance of actors' profile in which they can play the role of organisational communities by making relationships between logics either cooperative or competitive. Some literature argues for the importance of agency in respect to two logics (e.g. Smet and Jarzabkowski, 2013) but the importance of agency in constellations of logics has yet to be explored fully. Thornton et al. (2012) briefly raise the possibility of 'partial autonomy' of actors and agencies, and although there are already some institutionalists who have begun to argue for the importance of agencies (e.g. Delbridge and Edwards, 2013; Smet and Jarzabkowski, 2013), studies mainly focus on the dynamics between two logics rather than constellations of logics.

Another potential research area might be contemporary Japanese MNCs across different geographical locations. So far, there is a body of literature that discusses comparisons and contrasts between Japanese plants and local plants in a given location (e.g. Elger and Smith, 1994; 2005; Oliver and Wilkinson, 1988; 1992). There is less literature, however, discussing the complexity across geographical locations within a Japanese MNC. Abo (2015) strongly implies the relationality of how Japanese manufacturing practices are implemented across Asia and West. In Asia, they are relatively accepted in the same way as in Japan, but in the West, they are often rejected and resisted. These geographical contexts need to be better understood.

The last potential research concerns a methodological perspective. Many institutionalists focus on macro- and meso-level studies. These studies adopt mainly quantitative methods and or textual analysis, rather than participant observation. Their method goes along with identifying a reifying institutional tendency yet fails to pay attention to the meanings of actors. In line with the same argument, this tendency to focus on the macro and meso level is true for Japanese management scholars (e.g. Elger and Smith, 1994; 2005; Oliver and Wilkinson, 1988; 1992) with some exceptions (Graham, 1994; Delbridge, 1998). As Elger and Smith (2005) point out Western scholars lack 'area knowledge' of Japan, such as culture and languages. A quasi-ethnographic study needs to be pursued by scholars with area knowledge to provide nuanced, rich articulations of the meanings of actors.

Appendix

Table A.1 The history of JTHAI

Phases	Year	Events
Initiation	1985	Started joint venture with ThaiCo
	1989	Established sales representative in AmericaCo Thailand
	1995	Incorporated JTHAI (JTHAI)
		First Japanese president appointed
Stagnation	1997	Asian financial crisis occurred
		The company operated at a loss
		Second and third Japanese presidents appointed
Expansion	2002	The economy recovered and many Japanese manufacturers started to transfer their factories to Thailand
		The company generated profit
		Fourth and fifth Japanese presidents appointed
	2004	Reached more than 100 employees, hiring new graduates
	2006	Established the Valve Maintenance Service Centre in Rayong
		Changed organisational structure from functional to divisional (Thai managers appointed for the first time)
	2007	Established a sales office branch in Amata
	2010	Sixth Japanese president (who was hired from another Japanese company) appointed

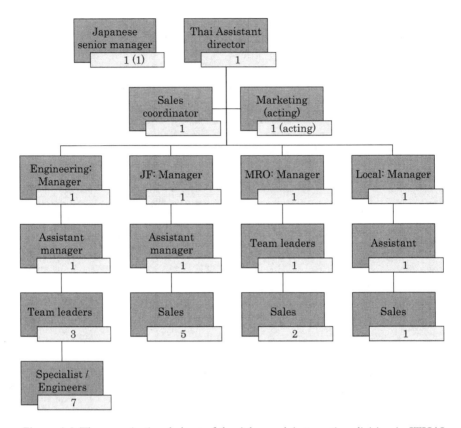

Figure A.1 The organisational chart of the Advanced Automation division in JTHAI

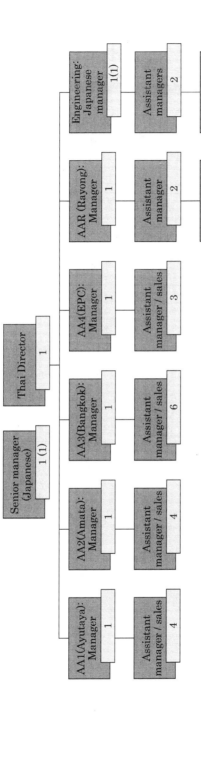

Figure A.2 The organisational chart of the Building Automation division in JTHAI

Table A.2 The history of JTAIW

Phases	Year	Events
Initiation	1969	Established a representative office in AmericaCo
	1997	Asian financial crisis
	1999	Incorporated JapanCo Taiwan; first Japanese president appointed
Expansion	2002	Started to generate profit by active sales to Japanese manufacturers in Taiwan; second Japanese president appointed
	2007	Third Taiwanese Japanese president appointed; expanded the business and recruited more than 10 employees, resulting in around 50 employees; caused accounting scandal and withdrew from his position
Stagnation	2009	Fourth Japanese president appointed (who had been the first president)
	2010	Fifth Japanese president appointed Management philosophy launched

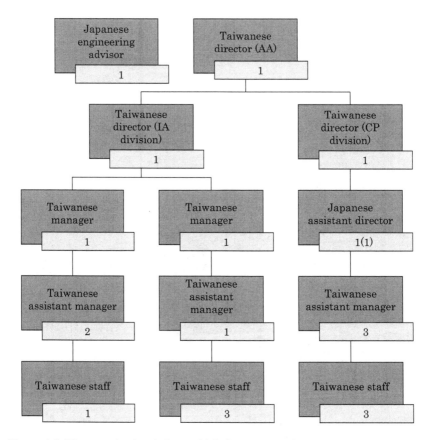

Figure A.3 The organisational chart of AA division in JTAIW

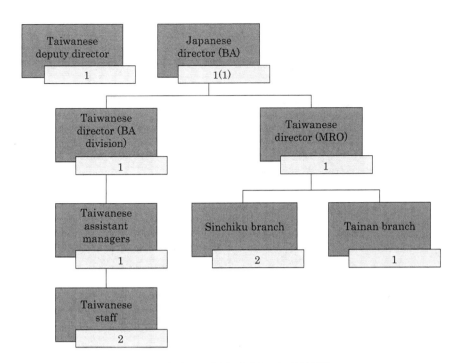

Figure A.4 The organisational chart of BA division in JTAIW

Table A.3 The history of JUSA

Phases	Year	Events
Initiation	-1996	Managed sales office in AmericaCo
	1996	Established Control Valve USA and first Japanese president appointed
	1998	Acquired an American valve manufacturer
	2001	Established Sensing Control another company
	2002	Second Japanese president appointed at Control Valve USA
Restart/Growth	2003	End of strategic alliance with AmericaCo
		Cleared the acquired American valve manufacturer
	2005	Third Japanese president appointed at JapanOldCo Control Valve USA
	2008	Financial crisis (Lehman shock)
	2009	Consolidated all subsidiaries into JUSA
	2010	First Japanese president appointed at JUSA
		American Biological company acquired and merged with
Expansion	2012	Second Japanese president appointed at JUSA
		American metre manufacturer acquired

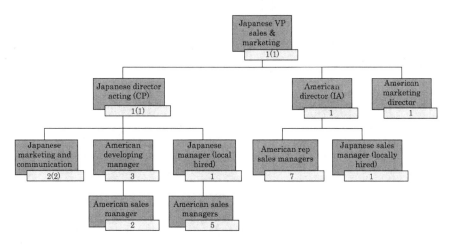

Figure A.5 The sales and marketing organisational chart in JUSA

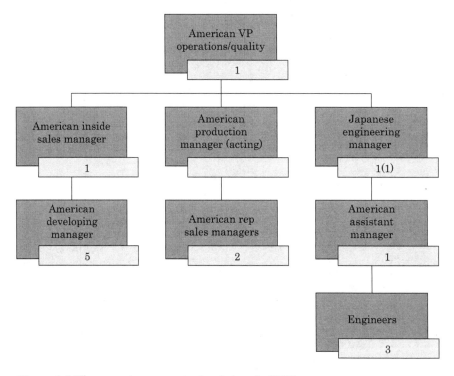

Figure A.6 The operations organisational chart in JUSA

Table A.4 The history of JEU

Phases	Year	Events
Initiation	1989	Sales representative of JapanCo established in AmericaCo Europe
	2001	JapanCo Europe established in Belgium
		First Japanese president appointed
	2003	Ended strategic alliance with AmericaCo
Expansion	2004	Second Japanese president appointed
		Expanded up to 15 employees
Stagnation	2008	Financial crisis occurred (Lehman shock)
	2009	Third Japanese president appointed (hired in the middle of his career)
		JEU from restructured from 15 to 8 employees, resulting in fierce resistance and confrontation
	2012	Fourth president appointed
		Started strategic initiative to expand business again

Bibliography

Abegglen, J. C. 1958. *The Japanese factory*. Tokyo, Japan: Nihon Keizai Shimbunsha.

Abercrombie, N., Hill, S. and Turner, B. S. 2000. *The Penguin dictionary of sociology*. 4th ed. Penguin.

Abo, T. 2015. Researching international transfer of the Japanese-style management and production system: Hybrid factories in six continents. *Asian Business & Management* 14(1), pp. 5–35.

Ackroyd, S., Burrell, G, Hughes, M. and Whitaker, A. 1988. The Japanisation of British industry? *Industrial Relations Journal* 19(1).

Agar, M. H. 1986. *Speaking of ethnography*. SAGE Publications (London).

Alvesson, M. 2009. At-home ethnography: Struggling with closeness and closure. In: Ybema, S., Yanow, D., Wels, H. and Kamsteeg, F. H. eds. *Organizational ethnography: Studying the complexity of everyday life*. pp. 156–174.

Anderson, K. H. and Hill, M. A. 1983. Marriage and labor market discrimination in Japan. *Southern Economic Journal* 49(4), pp. 941–953.

Asakawa, K., Kiyohiko, I, Rose, E. and Westney, D. E. 2013. Internationalization in Japan's service industries. *Asia Pacific Journal of Management* 30(4).

Atmiyanandana, V. and Lawler, J. J. 2003. Culture and management in Thailand. In: Warner, M. ed. *Culture and management in Asia*. London: Routledge, pp. 228–248.

Bae, J., Chen, S., Wan, T., Lawler, J. and Walumbba, F. 2003. Human resource strategy and firm performance in Pacific Rim countries. *The International Journal of Human Resource Management* 14(8).

Bae, K.-S., Chuma, H., Kato, T., Kim, D.-B. and Ohash, I. 2011. High performance work practices and employee voice: A comparison of Japanese and Korean workers. *Industrial Relations: A Journal of Economy and Society* 50(1), pp. 1–29.

Baker, C. 2004. Membership categorization and interview accounts. In: Silverman, D. ed. *Qualitative research: Theory, method and practice*. 2nd ed. London: Sage Publications, p. 378.

Battilana, J. and Dorado, S. 2010. Building sustainable hybrid organizations: the case of commercial microfinance organizations. *Academy of Management Journal* 53(6), pp. 1419–1440.

Beechler, S., Stephan, J., Puckik, V. and Campbell, N. 1996. Decision Making Localization and Decentralization in Japanese MNCs: Are there Costs of Leaving Local Managers Out of the Loop? *Working Paper Series: Center on Japanese Economy and Business: Graduate School of Business Columbia University*, Working Paper No. 101.

Beechler, S. L. and Bird, A. eds. 1999. *Japanese multinationals abroad: Individual and organizational learning (Japan Business and Economics Series)*. New York, p. 284.

Beechler, S. and Yang, J. Z. 1994. The transfer of Japanese-style management to American subsidiaries: Contingencies, constraints, and competencies. *Journal of International Business Studies* 25(3), pp. 467–491.

Bell, E. and Willmott, H. 2014. Editors' introduction: Qualitative research – themes and prospects. In: Bell, E. and Willmott, H. eds. *Qualitative research in business and management. Vol. I. Classical and contemporary studies*. Thousand Oaks, CA: Sage Publications Ltd.

Berger, P. and Luckman, T. 1966. *The Social Construction of Reality*. London: The Penguin Group.

Bhappu, A. D. 2000. The Japanese family: An institutional logic for Japanese corporate network and Japanese management. *Academy of Management Journal* 25(2), pp. 409–415.

Boxenbaum, E. and Jonsson, S. 2008. Isomorphism, diffusion and decoupling. In: Greenwood, R., Oliver, C., Sahlin, K. and Suddaby, R. eds. *The sage handbook of organizational institutionalism*. Thousand Oaks, CA: Sage Publications, pp. 78–98.

Brannen, M. Y. and Salk, J. E. 2000. Partnering across borders: Negotiating organizational culture in a German-Japanese joint venture. *Human Relations* 53(4), pp. 451–487.

Bryman, A. 2008. *Social research methods*. 3rd ed. New York: Oxford university press.

Bryman, A. and Bell, E. 2011. *Business research methods*. 3rd ed. New York: Oxford University Press.

Burrell, G. and Morgan, G. 1979. *Sociological paradigm and organisational analysis*. Vermont: Ashgate Publishing Company.

Chang, S. J. 1995. International expansion strategy of Japanese firms: Capability building through sequential entry. *Academy of Management Journal* 38(2), pp. 383–407.

Cho, J. and Trent, A. 2006. Validity in qualitative research revisited. *Qualitative Research* 6(3), pp. 319–340.

Chou, W.-C. G. 2003. Culture and management in Taiwan. In: Warner, M. ed. *Culture and management in Asia*. London: Routledge, pp. 210–227.

Chung, C.-N. and Luo, X. 2008. Institutional logics or agency costs: The influence of corporate governance models on business group restructuring in emerging economies. *Organization Science* 19(5), pp. 766–784.

Chung, W. K. and Hamilton, G. 2001. Social logic as business logic: Guanxi, trustworthiness and the embeddedness of Chinese business practices. In: Appelbaum, R. P., Feistiner, W.L.F. and Gessner, V. eds. *In rules and networks: The legal culture of global business transactions*. Oxford: Hart, pp. 302–349.

Cole, R. E. 1971. *Japanese blue collar: The changing tradition*. Oakland, CA: University of California Press.

Collinson, S. and Rugman, A. M. 2008. The regional nature of Japanese multinational business. *Journal of International Business Studies* 39(2), pp. 215–230.

Corradi, G., Gherardi, S. and Verzelloni, L. 2010. Through the practice lens: Where is the bandwagon of practice-based studies heading? *Management Learning* 41(3).

Delbridge, R. 1998. *Life on the line in contemporary manufacturing: The workplace experience of lean production and the 'Japanese' model*. New York: Oxford University Press.

Delbridge, R. and Edwards, T. 2007. Reflections on developments in institutional theory: Toward a relational approach. *Scandinavian Journal of Management* 23(2), pp. 191–205.

Delbridge, R. and Edwards, T. 2013. Inhabiting institutions: Critical realist refinements to understanding institutional complexity and change. *Organization Studies (online print)* 0(0), pp. 1–21.

DiMaggio, P. J. and Powell, W. W. 1983. The iron cage revisited: Institutional isomorphism and collective rationality. *American Sociological Review* 48(2), pp. 147–160.

DiMaggio, P. J. and Powell, W. W. 1991. The iron cage revisited: Institutional isomorphism and collective rationality. In: Powell, W. W. and DiMaggio, P. J. eds. *The new institutionalism in organizational analysis.* Chicago: University of Chicago Press, pp. 63-82.

Dollinger, M. J. 1988. Confucian ethics and Japanese management practices. *Journal of Business Ethics* 7(8), pp. 575–584.

Dore, R. 1973. *British factory – Japanese factory: The origins of national diversity in industrial relations.* London: Allen and Unwin.

Edwards, P., Ram, M., Gupta, S. S. and Tsai, C.-J. 2006. The structuring of working relationships in small firms: Towards a formal framework. *Organization* 13(5), pp. 701–724.

Elger, T. and Smith, C. eds. 1994. *Global Japanization? The transnational transformation of the labour process.* London, New York: Routledge.

Elger, T. and Smith, C. 2005. *Assembling work: Remaking factory regimes in Japanese multinationals in Britain.* New York: Oxford University Press.

Endo, T., Delbridge, R. and Morris, J. 2015. Does Japan still matter? Past tendencies and future opportunities in the study of Japanese firms. *International Journal of Management Reviews* 17(1), pp. 101–123.

Ferner, A. 1997. Country of origin effects and HRM in multinational companies. *Human Resource Management Journal* 7(1), pp. 19–37.

Fligstein, N. 1987. The intraorganizational power struggle: Rise of finance personnel to top leadership in large corporations, 1919–1979. *American Sociological Review* 52(1), pp. 44–58.

Foley, D. E. 2002. Critical ethnography: The reflexive turn. *International Journal of Qualitative Studies in Education* 15(4), pp. 469–490.

Friedland, R. 2012. God, Love and Other Good Reasons for Practice: Thinking Through Institutional Logics. In: *"Organizing Institutions: Creating, Enacting and Reacting to Institutional Logics" ABC network conference, Banff Springs Hotel, June 14–16.*

Friedland, R., Mohr, J., Roose, H. and Gardinali, P. 2014. The institutional logics of love: Measuring intimate life. *Theory and Society* 43(3–4), pp. 333–370.

Friedland, R. and Alford, R. R. 1991. Bringing society back in: Symbols, practices, and institutional contradictions. In: Powell, W. W. and DiMaggio, P. J. eds. *The new institutionalism in organizational analysis.* Chicago: Chicago Press, pp. 232–263.

Geertz, C. 1973. *The interpretation of cultures.* New York: Basic Books.

Geppert, M., Matten, D. and Walgenbach, P. 2006. Transnational institution building and the multinational corporation: An emerging field of research. *Human Relations* 59(11), pp. 1451–1465.

Giddens, A. 1976. *New rules of sociological method: A positive critique of interpretative sociologies.* London: Hutchinson.

Giddens, A. 1984. *The constitution of society: Introduction of the theory of structuration*. Cambridge: Polity Press.

Goerzen, A. and Makino, S. 2007. Multinational corporation internationalization in the service sector: A study of Japanese trading companies *Journal of International Business Studies* 38(7), pp. 1149–1169.

Goodrick, E. and Reay, T. 2011. Constellations of institutional logics changes in the professional work of pharmacists. *Work and Occupations* 38(3), pp. 372–416.

Graham, L. 1994. How does the Japanese model transfer the United States? A view from the line. In: Elger, T. and Smith, C. eds. *Global Japanization? The transnational transformation of the labour process*. London, New York: Routledge, pp. 123–151.

Greenwood, R., Diaz, A. M. and Li, S. X. 2010. The multiplicity of institutional logics and the heterogeneity of organizational responses. *Organization Science* 21(2), pp. 521–539.

Greenwood, R., Raynardb, M., Kodeihc, F., Micelottad, E. and Lounsburye, M. 2011. Institutional complexity and organizational responses. *The Academy of Management Annals* 5(1), pp. 317–371.

Greenwood, R. and Suddaby, R. 2006. Institutional entrepreneurship in mature fields: The big five accounting firms. *Academy of Management Journal* 49(1), pp. 27–48.

Hall, E. T. 1973. *The silent language*. New York: Doubleday.

Hallett, T. and Ventresca, M. J. 2006. Inhabited institutions: Social interactions and organizational forms in Gouldner's "patterns of industrial bureaucracy". *Theory and Society* 35(2), pp. 213–236.

Hatvany, N. and Pucik, V. 1981. An integrated management: Lessons from the Japanese experience. *Academy of Management Review* 6(3), pp. 469–480.

Hofstede, G. and Minkov, M. 2010. *Cultures and organizations: Software of the mind*. New York: McGraw Hill Professional.

ISHINO, I. 1953. The Oyabun-Kobun: A Japanese ritual kinship institution. *American Anthropologist* 55(5), pp. 695–707.

Karra, N., Tracey, P. and Phillips, N. 2006. Altruism and agency in the family firm: Exploring the role of family, kinship, and ethnicity. *Entrepreneurship Theory and Practice* 30(6), pp. 861–877.

Keizer, A., Umemura, M., Delbridge, R. and Morgan, G. 2012. Japanese Management 20 years on. *ESRC/ESRC Advanced Institute of Management Research Executive Briefing* [Online]. Available at http://www.aimresearch.org/uploads/File/Publications/Executive%20Briefings%202/AIM_Japan_EB_FINAL.pdf.

Kelle, U. 2004. Computer-assisted qualitative data analysis. In: Seale, C. ed. *Qualitative research practice*. Thousand Oaks, CA: Sage, pp. 443–459.

Keys, J. B. and Miller, T. R. 1984. The Japanese management theory jungle. *Academy of Management Review* 9(2), pp. 342–353.

Keys, J. B. and Miller, T. R. 1994. The Japanese management theory jungle-revisited. *Journal of Management* 20(2), pp. 373–402.

Kondo, D. K. 1990. *Crafting selves: Power, gender, and discourses of identity in a Japanese workplace*. Chicago: University of Chicago Press.

Kopp, R. 1994. International human resource policies and practices in Japanese, European, and United States multinationals. *Human Resource Management* 33(4), pp. 581–599.

Kopp, R. 1999. The rice-paper ceiling in Japanese companies: Why it exists and persists. In: Beechler, S. L. and Bird, A. eds. *Japanese multinationals abroad: Individual and organizational learning (Japan business and economics series)*. New York: OUP: USA, pp. 107–128.

Kostova, T., Roth, K. and Dacin, M. T. 2008. Institutional theory in the study of multinational corporations: A critique and new directions. *Academy of Management Review* 33(4), pp. 994–1006.

Lawrence, T., Suddaby, R. and Leca, B. 2011. Institutional work: Refocusing institutional studies of organization. *Journal of Management Inquiry* 20(1), pp. 52–58.

Lincoln, J. R., Olson, J., Hanada, M. 1978. Cultural effects on organizational structure: The case of Japanese firms in the United States. *American Sociological Review* 43(6), pp. 829–847.

Lincoln, Y. S. and Guba, E. G. 1985. *Naturalistic inquiry*. Thousand Oaks, CA: Sage.

Lounsbury, M. 2002. Institutional transformation and status mobility: The professionalization of the field of finance. *Academy Management Journal* 45(1), pp. 255–266.

Lounsbury, M. 2007. A tale of two cities: Competing logics and practice variation in the professionalizing of mutual funds. *Academy Management Journal* 50(2), pp. 289–307.

Marquis, C., Glynn, M. A. and Davis, G. F. 2007. Community isomorphism and corporate social action. *Academy of Management Review* 32(3), pp. 925–945.

Marquis, C. and Battilana, J. 2009. Acting globally but thinking locally? The enduring influence of local communities on organizations. *Research in Organizational Behavior* 29, pp. 283–302.

Marquis, C. and Lounsbury, M. 2007. vive la résistance: Competing logics and the consolidation of U.S. community banking. *Academy Journal of Management* 50(4), pp. 799–820.

Mason, J. 2002. *Qualitative researching*. 2nd ed. London: Sage.

Meyer, J. W. and Rowan, B. 1977. Institutionalized organizations: Formal structure as myth and ceremony. *American Journal of Sociology* 83(2), pp. 340–363.

Miller, D., Lee, J., Chang, S. and Breton-Miller, I. 2009. Filling the institutional void: The social behavior and performance of family vs non-family technology firms in emerging markets. *Journal of International Business Studies* 40(5), pp. 802–817.

Miller, J. and Glassner, B. 1997. The 'inside' and the 'outside': Finding reality in interviews. In: Silverman, D. ed. *Qualitative research: Theory, method and practice*. 2nd ed. London: Sage, pp. 99–112.

Mutch, A. 2009. Weber and church governance: Religious practice and economic activity. *The Sociological Review* 57(4), pp. 586–607.

Nordqvist, M. and Melin, L. 2010. Entrepreneurial families and family firms. *Entrepreneurship & Regional Development* 22(3–4), pp. 211–239.

Oliver, C. 1991. Strategic responses to institutional processes. *Academy of Management Review* 16(1), pp. 145–179.

Oliver, N. and Wilkinson, B. 1988. *The Japanization of British industry*. Oxford, Blackwell.

Oliver, N. and Wilkinson, B. 1992. *The Japanization of British industry*. 2nd ed. Oxford, Blackwell.

Pascale, R. T. and Athos, A. G. 1982. *The art of Japanese management*. New York: Penguin.

Rao, H., Monin, P. and Durand, R. 2003. Institutional change in Toque Ville: Nouvelle Cuisine as an identity movement in French gastronomy. *American Journal of Sociology* 108(4), pp. 795–843.

Reay, T. and Hinings, C. R. 2005. The recomposition of an organizational field: health care in Alberta. *Organization Studies* 26(3), pp. 351–384.

Reay, T. and Hinings, C. R. 2009. Managing the rivalry of competing institutional logics. *Organization Studies* 30(6), pp. 629–652.

Rinehart, J., Robertson, D., Huxley, C. and Wareham, J. 1994. Reunifying conception and execution of work under Japanese production management? A Canadian case study. In: Elger, T. and Smith, C. eds. *Global Japanization? The transnational transformation of the labour process.* London, New York: Routledge.

Schatzki, T. R. et al. 2001. *The practice turn in contemporary theory.* Routledge.

Schonberger, R. 1982. *Japanese manufacturing techniques: Nine hidden lessons in simplicity.* New York: Free Press London: Collier Macmillan.

Silverman, D. 1970. *The theory of organizations.* 3rd ed. London: Heinemann.

Silverman, D. 2006. *Interpreting qualitative data.* 3rd ed. London: Sage Publications.

Smets, M. and Jarzabkowski, P. 2013. Reconstructing institutional complexity in practice: A relational model of institutional work and complexity. *Human Relations (online print)* 0(0), pp. 1–31.

Suddaby, R., Elsbach, K., Greenwood, R. Meyer, J. and Zilber, T. 2010. Organizations and their institutional environments—bringing meaning, values, and culture back in: introduction to the special research forum. *Academy of Management Journal* 53(6), pp. 1234–1240.

Suddaby, R., Viale, T. and Gendron, Y. 2012. Institutional Reflexivity: The Role of the Individual in Institutional Work. 1st European Theory Development Workshop at Grenoble School of Management, France.

Sumihara, N. 1999. Roles of knowledge and "Cross-knowledge" in creating a third culture: An example of performance appraisal in a Japanese corporation in New York. In: Beechler, S. L. and Bird, A. eds. *Japanese multinationals abroad: Individual and organizational learning (Japan business and economics series).* New York: OUP: USA, p. 284.

Thomas, A. B. 2004. *Research skills for management studies.* 2nd ed. New York: Routledge.

Thornton, P. H. 2002. The rise of the corporation in a craft industry: conflict and conformity in institutional logics. *Academy of Management Journal* 45(1), pp. 81–101.

Thornton, P. H. 2004. *Markets from culture: Institutional logics and organizational decisions in higher education publishing.* Stanford, CA: Stanford University Press, pp. 81–101.

Thornton, P. H. et al. 2005. Institutional logics and institutional change in organizations: Transformation in accounting, architecture, and publishing. In: Thornton, P. H. and Jones, C. eds. *Transformation in cultural industries (Research in the sociology of organizations).* Vol. 23. Emerald Group Publishing, pp. 125–170.

Thornton, P. H., Jones, C. and Kury, K. 2012. *The institutional logics perspective: A new approach to culture, structure and process.* New York: Oxford University Press.

Thornton, P. H. and Ocasio, W. 1999. Institutional logics and the historical contingency of power in organizations: Executive succession in the higher education publishing industry. *American Journal of Sociology* 105(3), pp. 801–843.

Turnbull, P. 1986. The 'Japanisation' of production and industrial relations at Lucas Electrical. *Industrial Relations Journal* 17(3), pp. 193–206.

Vogel, E. F. 1979. *Japan as number one: Lessons for America.* Cambridge, MA: Harvard University Press.

Voronov, M., Clercq, D. and Hinings, C.R.. 2013. Institutional complexity and logic engagement: An investigation of Ontario fine wine. *Human Relations* 66(12), pp. 1563–1596.

Waldorff, S. B., Reay, T. and Goodrick, E. 2013. A tale of two countries: How different constellations of logics impact action. In: Lounsbury, M. and Boxenbaum, E. eds. *Institutional logics in action (Research in the sociology of organizations)*. 39A, Emerald Group Publishing, pp. 99–129.

Watanabe, S. 2000. The Japan model and the future of employment and wage systems. *International Labour Review* 139(3), pp. 307–333.

Weber, M. 2010. *The protestant ethic and the spirit of capitalism*. Createspace.

Westney, D. E. 1987. Internal and external linkages in the MNC: The case of R&D subsidiaries in Japan. In: *The management of the MNC*. Brussel.

Westney, D. E. 1999. Changing perspectives on the organization of Japanese multinational companies. In: Beechler, S. L. and Bird, A. eds. *Japanese multinationals abroad: individual and organizational learning (Japan business and economics series)*. New York: OUP: USA. p. 284.

Westphal, J. D. and Zajac, E. J. 1998. The symbolic management of stockholders: Corporate governance reforms and shareholder reactions. *Administrative Science Quarterly* 43(1), pp. 127–153.

Whitley, R., Morgan, G., Kelly, W. and Sharpe, D.. 2003. The changing Japanese multinational: Application, adaptation and learning in car manufacturing and financial services. *Journal of Management Studies* 40(3), pp. 643–672.

Williams, K., Mitusi, I. and Haslan, C. 1994. How far from Japan? A case study of Japanese press shop practice and management. In: Elger, T. and Smith, C. eds. *Global Japanization? The transnational transformation of the labour process*. London, New York: Routledge, pp. 60–90.

Yin, R. K. 2003. *Case study research: Data and methods*. London: Sage.

Yuen, E. C. and Kee, H. T. 1993. Headquarters, host-culture and organizational influences on HRM policies and practices. *Management International Review* 33(4), pp. 361–383.

Zilber, T. B. 2002. Institutionalization as an interplay between actions, meanings, and actors: The case of a rape crisis center in Israel. *The Academy of Management Journal* 45(1), pp. 234–254.

Zilber, T. B. 2006. The work of the symbolic in institutional processes: Translations of rational myths in Israeli high tech. *The Academy of Management Journal* 49(2), pp. 281–303.

Zucker, L. G. 1977. The role of institutionalization in cultural persistence. *American Sociological Review* 42(5), pp. 726–743.

Zussman, R. 2004. People in places. *Qualitative Sociology* 27(4), pp. 351–363.

Index